GOD'S WAY WITH MEN

GOD'S WAY WITH MEN

A Study of the Relationship Between God and Man in Providence, "Miracle," and Prayer

by

NORMAN PITTENGER

JUDSON PRESS
VALLEY FORGE

Copyright © Norman Pittenger 1969

8170–0465–3

Library of Congress Catalog Card No.
71–86853

PRINTED IN GREAT BRITAIN FOR JUDSON PRESS, VALLEY FORGE,
PA. 19481 BY EBENEZER BAYLIS AND SON, LIMITED, THE TRINITY
PRESS, WORCESTER, AND LONDON

ACKNOWLEDGEMENTS

The extract from *The Glory of Man* by David Jenkins is reproduced here by kind permission of the publishers, S.C.M. Press Ltd.

Acknowledgement is due for permission to quote from the song "She Loves You": words and music by John Lennon and Paul McCartney © copyright 1963 Northern Songs Limited; and from the song "Someone, Someone", reproduced by kind permission of Burlington Music Company Limited.

AUTHOR'S PREFACE

AUTHOR'S PREFACE

A preface provides opportunity for comments of a preliminary sort. One of them has to do with the style in which this book is written. It is intended not for the theological expert but for the educated layman and the ordinary parish priest. It has seemed best to write it, therefore, in a style which may be called *popular* and *personal*. That is, I have eschewed so far as possible detailed theological terminology, save where this can be readily understood or where any dictionary will provide a clue to the meaning of words; and I have introduced many illustrations and analogies, drawn from common experience, to indicate the "point" at many places in my argument. I have also been personal – some may think too personal – in the expression of ideas and opinions; on occasion I have "let myself go" in the statement of views that seem to me of importance for us today. My reason for this personal quality in writing is that our contemporaries expect, rightly I think, that any author on matters of faith shall honestly and precisely say what he himself thinks. In this book I have tried to do just that.

When Father Thornton first asked me to contribute to the series he suggested that a discussion of the Christian belief in "providence" might be useful. As I thought about the matter, it became clear to me that providence is only satisfactorily considered in the more general context of God's way with his world and with men and that such a context demands that other matters also be dealt with:

namely, "miracle", a specifically religious concept having to do with particular occasions when God's presence and power are felt with singular intensity; and prayer, or communion with God, in intentional and fully conscious direction of the human personality towards its divine creator.

Further thought brought me to feel that one cannot speak about a relationship without giving due attention to the terms included in it: in this case, who *God* is and who *man* is. Still working backwards, so to say, I then realised that one can only speak in a Christian fashion about God and man, in their relationship one with the other, when one has come to grips with the significance of him whom Origen was the first to call "God-Man": that is, that One in whom God discloses himself by act in genuinely human life, doing this in a fashion so intimate, adequate, and decisive that the word "Incarnation" may justly be applied to the action of God in that instance.

The conclusions which I reached in this manner explain the development of the book's argument. Beginning with Jesus Christ himself, I move on to consider the nature of God and of man, and the relationship between them both by creation and the "new life" in Christ Jesus; only then do I deal with providence, "miracle", and prayer. I am under no illusions about what German writers would call the "programmatic character" of this discussion. Each chapter could have been expanded into a whole book. But there is something to be said for bringing each of these topics into unity with the others; for if it be true, as I am sure it is, that the entire Christian enterprise is "organic" in nature, a whole with interpenetrating and interrelated parts, then it is useful to attempt to see something of that wholeness. I hope that I have managed to convey to the reader my own vision of the "organic" quality of the Christian reality.

In order not to break the continuity of the argument, yet not to leave the reader in doubt about certain related topics, I have appended to some of the chapters notes which consider how I understand the modern use of Scripture for theological purposes, the importance of seeing the natural order as well as history as a sphere of the divine activity, and Christian moral principles as they flow from and are associated with Christian faith in God as Love. I trust that these brief notes will meet some of the questions which those who read the book might wish to raise.

It remains for me to express, once again, my indebtedness to Father Thornton for his invitation, and my gratitude for many suggestions from other friends, especially those in Cambridge with whom I have been able to discuss theological points relevant to the various subjects dealt with in this book. Some of my colleagues at King's College have helped in ways of which they are probably quite unconscious, not least by putting up with me during the period in which I have been working on this book. If there were a "dedication", I should wish to name four of those friends: Alec Vidler, former Dean of King's College; David Edwards, the present Dean; Peter Avery, Fellow of the College; and William Leah, former chaplain and now a minor canon at Westminster. The affection of such fellow Christians helps one to know what Christian love is all about; and I am unspeakably grateful to them for that never-failing affection.

King's College
Cambridge   Norman Pittenger

CONTENTS

CHAPTER ONE

The Self-Disclosure of God in Act

The heart of Christianity is Jesus Christ.

To say that may seem to be to say something so obvious that it is only a truism. But it is not *just* a truism; nor is its meaning so obvious as might appear at first sight. For what is meant by that name, "Jesus Christ"?

For the past half century, the meaning of that term has been taken to be that Jesus Christ is the unique revelation of God in the sense that in him, and in him only, do we receive any valid knowledge of the character and purpose of the divine reality. Those who have maintained this position have been called, and sometimes have called themselves, "neo-orthodox". They have tended to deny, or at least to minimise in an extreme way, the enterprise which used to be called "natural theology"; this claim, that something important may be known about God from man's more general experience and thought, has been dismissed as blasphemous and absurd. Furthermore, they have written, on occasion, as if even the Jewish faith reflected and witnessed in the Old Testament is meaningless save as it receives its significance from Jesus alone. This position, in its various forms, is of course extreme. But it has its approximations in a great many milder kinds of "christo-monism", to use a word which has been coined to describe the views enunciated in much of Karl Barth's writing.

On the other hand, many good people and some theologians have found Jesus Christ to be the heart of Christianity in a quite different sense. They have not concerned themselves with what used to be called his "divinity", for (in at least some instances) they have been convinced that all talk about God is either unverifiable or actually nonsensical. Their main interest has been in Jesus as "the Man for others", whose abiding value for us is that he is "the place where we stand", or the person from whom "freedom becomes contagious", or the "pattern of true manhood". In other words, the heart of Christianity is indeed Jesus Christ; but Jesus Christ is taken to be the name of the greatest, the best, the wisest, the most penetrating of men, who in his own lifetime and in his own way acted out upon the stage of history the truth which should instruct and inform the rest of us. Why *this* Man, rather than some other, should thus be singled out is not always clear; none the less, there he is – and it is he who is the "type" of all genuine manhood, however different may be the circumstances under which men in succeeding ages may find themselves obliged to follow him.

But the point of the name Jesus Christ, for the central and continuing tradition of Christian faith, has really been neither of these alternatives. One feels impelled to say, although to say it in just this fashion is to beg the question, that "authentic" Christianity has had a quite different way of understanding Jesus Christ. It is that way, I am myself convinced, which is the right way to understand him; and this first chapter is intended to make clear certain important elements in that "right way".

What *is* the way which avoids both of the alternatives

just mentioned? Very briefly, it is to regard Jesus Christ as
that One – and I put it thus vaguely because I do not wish
to prejudge certain highly important issues in christological discussion – in whom *both* God and man are present, because *both* God and man are at work. More than
this, it is to insist that Jesus Christ is not the *only* person or
place in which God is met and known. In language familiar to Anglicans, for they recall words often used by
William Temple, he is the correction but he is also the
crown of God's never-failing activity in the world; he does
not deny nor negate, but he fulfils and puts in right perspective, all that has been disclosed about God in Jewish
faith, in non-Christian and non-Jewish religions, in the
secular world, in the natural order, and wherever and
however else God has permitted men to learn something
about him.

In other words, this way of regarding Jesus Christ is
neither christo-centric in the Barthian sense nor Jesu-
centric in the humanistic sense. If it has any centre, that
centre is in God himself – it is theo-centric. Yet it speaks
about God *in* Christ; for the heart of Christianity *is* Jesus
Christ in the profoundly serious sense that Jesus Christ is
taken as the distinctive and decisive norm for all that is
said about God. Again, it sees Jesus Christ as also the truth
about man and about every man; but it sees him as being
that truth precisely because he is supremely and especially
the "Man for God". He is indeed also the "Man for
others"; but that is the fact only because in the concrete
actuality of his human existence he is the enactment of the
reality of manhood *vis-à-vis* God.

This way of regarding Jesus Christ, this way of understanding the meaning of the statement that he is the heart
of Christianity, has been worked out in a variety of ways

2

during the course of Christian history. Such New Testament assertions as St. Paul's "in him dwelleth all the fulness of the Godhead bodily" (Col. 2.9), or the Johannine
"the Word was made flesh" (John 1.14), indicate to us the
beginnings of this process. Origen's use of the phrase "God-
Man" to describe Jesus Christ helps us along the way. The
Alexandrine "substance" christology and the Antiochene
christology of will are further signs of this development. It
is not the purpose of this book to engage in detailed christological discussion; my point here is only to say that in
all their rich diversity the Christian Church's differing
christologies have pointed towards a mysterious inter-
penetration of God and man in this One to whom men
have been drawn as their Lord. Somehow, in this particular historical existence, God and man are together in a
peculiarly intensive manner – so intimate, so interpenetrating, indeed, that God and man together in him are no
longer to be spoken of as "they" but as "he".

The precise nature of that personal unity, which enables
us to say "he" and to mean not God *only* nor man *only* but
God and man together there, has been the occasion of
great debate among theologians. We have already referred
by implication to the classic case – the difference between
the Alexandrine theologians who sought to state the nature
of the unity in substantial terms, derived from prevalent
philosophical notions familiar to their thinking, and the
Antiochene theologians who sought to state the nature of
the unity in terms drawn from categories like "will",
"good pleasure", "obedience", and "grace". In my own
judgement, the Antiochenes were right and the Alexand-
rines wrong; but that is neither here nor there. The significant emphasis for our purpose is that *both* of them were
anxious, above all else, to guarantee the full reality of God-

head *and* at the same time the full reality of manhood in the One whom both worshipped and adored as Lord and Master. They were convinced that if in any way the full reality of God's presence and act in Jesus were doubted or reduced, the Christian experience of new life from God through him would be denied. They were also convinced that if the full reality of manhood were doubted or reduced, the same experience would also be denied. And it was equally their conviction that if the full reality of God and the full reality of man were not in Jesus so entirely at one that there was no chance of their becoming "unstuck" (to put it in a vulgar modern word), the Christian experience could be nothing more than incidental to a given man or accidental in the course of history.

Something like that which the last paragraph has tried to express is at the core of the christological discussion, not only in the patristic period about which we have just written but also in every age in which Christians find themselves impelled to reckon with what it means to speak of Jesus Christ as "the heart of Christianity".

Now despite the recent questioning of Christianity as constituting a "revelation" of God, the patent truth is that the intention of Christian faith has always been to see in Jesus Christ precisely such a disclosure – but not of God alone; of man also. Of course the revelation is given in activity. This is the continuing Hebraic note in sound Christian thought. And in ages when that note has been muted there has been the danger that Jesus Christ will be regarded as "revealing" only in the sense that in him, so to say, the veil is withdrawn and we can *see*, but yet not be deeply affected by what goes on there. One of the recoveries which we may associate with renewed study of biblical thinking is right here: we now know that for biblical writers the way in which God wills to disclose himself to his human children is chiefly through what he *does* — or, in a phrase now so often used that it has become hackneyed, "through his 'mighty acts' ". That is why this chapter is entitled "The Self-Disclosure of God in Act".

Yet it *is* self-disclosure. In other words, it reveals something to those for whom the act was "determined, dared, and done", in Christopher Smart's grand phrase. So it is that we have been given, in the event which was Jesus Christ (that is, in "act"), a disclosure of God's own nature and of God's own purpose — or, as we must phrase it for the special concern of this book, "God's way with men". But at the same time, and by the same token, we have also been given a disclosure of *man*, man as God created him to be and as God intends him to be; we have been told, not in words but in concrete activity, what is the *truth* about man, and not about man generically but about each and every man including our own selves. In Jesus Christ there is enacted in human terms, decisively, "*God's* way with men"; there is also enacted in those same terms, *man's* proper way with God.

But what has this christological excursus to do with the subject of this book? The reply, in words St. Paul used in a very different context, is quite clear: "Much every way" (Rom. 3.2).

For this book is concerned with God's way with men, with particular reference to the fellowship or communion between them, the providential working of God in human life, the moments in their relationship in which fresh and unexpected things happen (miscalled in conventional theology by the unhappy word "miracle"), and the point and practice of prayer. In concerning itself with such matters, it must necessarily concern itself also with man himself, in his divinely intended nature and act. To speak of a relationship, as we must do, is of necessity to speak of both terms in that relationship. How can we hope to come to grips with the question of God and man in fellowship, of the sense in which men thus related to God are aware of God's "hand upon them", of the significance of the moments when God's presence and power are uniquely experienced, and of the intentional and conscious direction of a man to God, unless we know *whom we are talking about*?

A Christian has only one way of knowing this, in the deepest possible sense of the word "know". Whatever else he may have come to believe about God, for example, the final appeal for him must always be to that focal moment in human history when God acted decisively. Whatever he may believe about himself through the many avenues of knowledge open to him, he must always appeal to that same focal moment when he wishes to see the truth about himself, deep underneath surface appearances and passing fancies. That is part of what it means to *be* a Christian: it means to have that kind of reference for one's thinking as well as for one's doing.

Now one of the tragedies in Christian thinking, especially when it is consciously theological in its intention, is that this reference has not always been made. Professor Whitehead once remarked, in words that lately have been brought to our attention through their use by Professor Donald MacKinnon in some recent widely acclaimed broadcasts, that something very odd happened during the early days of the Christian Church. The "Galilean vision", with which Christianity began, tended to get somewhat dim; and in its place ideas of God's character and mode of operation in his world were introduced, whose origin was quite different. "The Church attributed to God that which belonged exclusively to Caesar," Whitehead said; in other words, the authority and near omnipotence claimed by the Roman emperors was predicated of God in an eminent sense. In consequence he was seen as being essentially a "ruler in might", rather than the Love which had been disclosed in Jesus Christ. Again, the impressive picture of the oriental despot, whose subjects cringed before him in lowly submission and whose behaviour was arbitrary and unpredictable, took the place of the picture of the faithful Father of his human children. Finally, from a misuse of the ancient Jewish prophetic stress on God's righteousness, God came to be thought of as what Whitehead called "a ruthless moralist", instead of the kind of Love which (in Whitehead's own words) "is a little oblivious to morals". When with this was coupled the passionate Greek desire to reach to an "unmoved Mover", who would be the explanation of the world yet would not himself be involved in the world, the mischief was done.

I am not interested here in how far Whitehead's analysis is entirely justified; doubtless there is a good deal of exaggeration in it and certainly throughout Christian history there have been many thinkers who have combated, in one way or another, the tendencies he described. My point is only that this has been the *direction* of much theological discussion, especially in respect to the particular topics with which in this book we are dealing. It seems to me very plain that a considerable amount of traditional Christian teaching about "miracle", for example, has been complicated, confused, and even rendered well-nigh incredible by ideas of God's way of working in the world which are not reconcilable with what is revealed about him in Jesus Christ. Of course there has been an additional factor here

— the survival even in our own day of deistic ideas about
how God is related to the world; yet even these have their
parallels in some of the earlier notions which the Church's
teachers were persuaded to adopt. As to prayer and its
meaning, the situation is even more obvious. For what
Dean Inge once styled, in an acid phrase, "pestering the
deity" has all too often been assumed to be the point of
praying; petition, and that of an extremely crude kind,
has been taken out of its rightful context and exalted in
such a way that it was not entirely a parody when a friend
remarked, "Prayer is bringing to God's attention what he
has overlooked and so insisting upon getting one's way
with him that he can only grant one's requests." And
providence has been reduced either to God's providing
comfort for those who happen to please him or his arrang-
ing (in an illustration once employed by G. K. Chesterton
in a bitter attack on such a cheap view of the matter) that
banana-skins shall be placed conveniently, so that a man
whom God likes can slip and fall on one of them, thus
sparing himself from entering a bus which a few minutes
later will plunge down a decline and bring death to all the
passengers.

What is more, communion or fellowship with God has
not infrequently been taken to mean, on God's part, a
remarkable and unlovely "condescension"; while on
man's part, it has suggested that we should consider ourselves inhuman, pleasing God by thinking of ourselves as
"worms and no man", thus denying both the image of
God in which we were created and also God's unfailing
working in us to bring us to the point where we earnestly
seek to be related to him as his "fellow-workers". Lest it be
thought here that I am deprecating humility and rever-
ence, let it be said at once that both of these are right and

necessary in the God-man relationship, for we are indeed
not only finite but sinful. Yet this need not imply, and for
a Christian ought not to imply, that we adopt what has
been styled the "Uriah Heep mentality", offering ourselves as doormats upon which, presumably, God will
delight to tread.

The last few paragraphs of our discussion may seem
unduly excited. I admit the excitement, but I reject the
use of the adjective. For what is at stake here is something
of enormous importance in the Christian enterprise; and
the amount of harm that has been done to countless men
and women by such erroneous teaching, or by such mistaken ideas derived from inadequate teaching, is appalling. What makes it so much worse is that these things
need never have been, had those who teach and those who
learn taken with utmost seriousness the self-disclosure of
God in act, supremely in Jesus Christ, and what this has
to tell us about God and about man.

If it be said, "let us not exaggerate", it can be replied,
"neither let us minimise". The harm has been done and
it has been an incalculable harm. We have every reason
to be thankful that by the movement of the Holy Spirit, as
I believe it to be, we are coming to have a change of attitude. For a variety of causes we are more and more realis-
ing that our thoughts about God must be in accord with
that "mind . . . which was also in Christ Jesus" (Phil. 2.5)
– and not only in his own self-awareness but in the totality
of all that he did; and that the same must be true of our
thought about human nature and its capacities. It would
be preposterous to claim that we in our generation are so
much "wiser than our fathers" that we possess the whole
truth. On the other hand, it would be wrong, and sub-
Christian, not to recognise that God's Holy Spirit, "taking

of the things of Christ", has brought us to see *some* of the things which an earlier generation did not see. There is no need to condemn our ancestors for not knowing what they did not know; they, like us, were men of their own time and did the best they could with what was available to them. So must we. And one of the things now available to us is the renewal of insight into the biblical way of thinking about God, while at the same time we have been enabled to use more seriously the conviction that God is indeed love – such love as is active in Jesus Christ for "us men and for our wholeness".

Let us sum up, before we move on to the next chapter. In Jesus Christ, there is both the activity of God, initiating and unfailing, and the activity of man, responding and obeying in faith with love. Those two activities are united in him, in a personal fashion, so that in the concrete event of Jesus Christ both are brought together as intimately and inseparably as can be conceived. Because this is the case, we are given an awareness of what God is and what he is "up to" in his world, and of his nature and his way; we are also given an understanding of who we are, we men who live in this world and under these human conditions from which we cannot escape and in which we must work out our destiny. In being given that double awareness, we are enabled to have some awareness also of the relationship between God and man – a relationship of communion for which we were created, which it is God's intention that we shall enjoy, and apart from which human existence is trivial and frustrated, however much self-styled humanists of a secularistic variety may say otherwise.

The heart of Christianity is indeed Jesus Christ. But what is more, Jesus Christ is also at the heart of the whole relationship between God and man. That is the Christian claim, nobly stated for us by one great English divine only lately rediscovered. Frederick Denison Maurice saw this, insisted upon it, and wrote both his *Kingdom of Christ* and his *Theological Essays* to bring it home to his own generation. As Maurice declared, Christ is "the head" of every man, as he is also the supreme and adequate revelation of God for every man.

CHAPTER TWO

Who God Is

We have entitled this chapter "*Who* God Is", not "*What* God Is". And the choice of the word "who", rather than "what", indicates immediately that God is in some profoundly serious sense *personal*. In what sense, we shall discuss later. But from the Christian point of view, as we have sought to present it in the last chapter, it is impossible to think of God in any way which would regard him as *less* than the one specimen in his creation which we know well — namely, ourselves.

So we begin by saying that whatever else God may be, he is One who has with his human children relations that are more like those which we have with one another than they are like those which obtain between sticks and stones, between men and trees, or between dogs and cats. Furthermore, we say that *in himself*, so far as we dare presume to speak of such a mystery, he is *more* like us in the kind of nature which is his than he is like the nature which can be attributed to those sticks, stones, trees, and even dogs or cats. Indeed God should be thought of as "thou".

Now one of the real difficulties with much that has traditionally been said about God is precisely here: it has tended to talk of him, in his essential nature, in the neuter, as "what" rather than "who". Despite the fact that the phrase frequently attributed to St. Thomas Aquinas, *ens realissimum*, is not his own but comes from the eighteenth century, where it was employed by Kant and some of those who went before him, the truth is that a good deal of scholastic thought about God has been along those "neuter" lines. Aquinas himself spoke of God as "being existing in itself" — *esse in se subsistens*. (Perhaps we should have said, not "existing" but "subsisting", although at this point the difference is immaterial.) *Esse* does not necessarily carry a "neuter" implication, of course, but as it has been used that implication seems almost inevitable. What is said about God in a more personal sense must then be said as an adjective modifying the *esse*. To use Ian T. Ramsey's idiom, the basic *model* is the abstract noun "being", with its neuter suggestions; the *qualifier* is "personal"; and so we get "personal being" as the meaning of the term God. There is a sense in which this usage is correct, as we shall see; but it is apparent that to talk in this way can be highly dangerous, for it may lead us to think that really, in the most real sense (*realissimum*, as we might put it), God is substantively "that which is". The typical scholastic line is to begin by talking about the *isness* of God, "that which is", "being itself"; and *then* to go on to say whatever can be said about the personalising of God. Yet the deliverance of Holy Scripture, as a witness to divine self-revelation, and the reality of the meeting with God disclosed in act in Jesus Christ, as well as the continuing experience of Christians and others, demand that we should work the other way round: *first* God is known as being in personal relationship with his children and hence as being himself in some serious fashion personal; *then*, and only then, is he thought about in terms of those "metaphysical compliments" which Professor

Whitehead said that theologians are always paying him.

I am well aware of the presence in the world of Buddhists and others who claim to have an "experience" of that which is *not* personal. I know about the Hindu way of talking of an impersonal "Brahman" which is more ultimate than all the manifestations in quasi-personalised and even over-personalised avatars or representations of deity. But we are speaking in this book of the *Christian* faith; and we are beginning our consideration of the questions with which this book is concerned, with the insistence that "the heart of Christianity is Jesus Christ". The God *of* Jesus Christ, the God *in* Jesus Christ, is not "being itself" or "that which is", in the first place certainly (although I am not saying, at this point, whether in the second or third place those phrases may be or may not be applicable); he is the personalised God who lives with men, works with men, speaks with men. God is "he", not "that".

It is plain enough that an excessive emphasis on this picture of God as personal, without the balancing considerations which presently will be introduced, can lead to dangerous and tragic misunderstanding. We are all familiar with the "great big Man up in the skies" idea, which the Bishop of Woolwich has lately been torpedoing. There is no reason to think of God in *that* way; and we must constantly be on our guard lest our "images" tend in that unfortunate direction. Yet I am frank to say that if one were obliged to choose – as, of course, one is not – between "the great big Man" and "a great big Thing", in one's thinking about God, I should not have the slightest hesitation in choosing the former. I say this as a Christian, of course; and my reason for saying it is that to my mind the "big Thing" picture is untrue to the deepest instincts and

the most profound realities of my own religious life, as
well as to the kind of portrayal of God which I find in
Holy Scripture and with which I am familiar from my
historical and personal knowledge of Jesus Christ. The
"big Man" is a mistaken image, to be sure—very seriously
mistaken, very dangerous, very likely to lead one into all
kinds of absurdity. But it is not the total *contradiction* of
everything which is most real to me as a Christian, as I
find the "big Thing" image to be.

I propose, then, that we begin our discussion of "who
God is" with a recognition that, in Christian faith, he is
at least personal – and I do not say "super-personal", for
the word at once suggests to us *im*personal, however much
we may wish to avoid this error. What does it mean to be
"personal"?

First of all, I believe, it means that the One we call by
that adjective is possessed of awareness and self-awareness.
Obviously God's kind of awareness is not precisely the
same as ours, limited as ours must be by the physiological
concomitants of consciousness. Nor would he be limited by
the kind of psychological process which is ours; notice that
I say "kind", because there is no real reason to suppose
that there is not a processive quality in God and that what
we may style his "consciousness" (although that is perhaps
an unfortunate word to use) may very well have the before-
and-after aspect which for us is part of our awareness.
Indeed I should wish to claim that there *is* in God this
kind of temporality – but more about that later on.

Not only awareness, but self-awareness . . . God not
only "knows" that which is not himself but he also knows
himself. What this might mean in God I do not know and
it would be absurd as well as blasphemous to claim that I
do. But it means at least that he knows his own "mind", as

we say of ourselves. And this leads us to the next element
in the constitution of "personality". It is purposive. A
personal being is distinguished from an impersonal one by
the possibility he possesses of making plans and then acting
upon them. Sticks and stones do not possess this, in any
sense which is identical with ours – although I believe that
there are very remote analogies throughout the creation,
down to what we describe as the "lowest levels" of matter-
in-motion or (in more modern scientific terms) energy-in-
process. Even at this lowest level, there can be and must
be a kind of grasping of what has gone before and using of
what is at hand, with some sort of *aim*; but down there, and
for a long way "up", this is not consciously entertained.
In the higher animals, we are told these days, there are the
rudiments of such purposiveness, just as there are the rudiments of self-awareness. Doubtless that is true enough; but
the point is that the intensity of these which we know in
ourselves is so different in degree that it effectively operates
as a difference in kind – and it points to the highest degree
of self-awareness with purpose, which we may predicate of
God himself. Let us observe, too, that purposiveness also
suggests some kind of temporality in God.

Again, to be personal means that one can communicate
with others, in a relatively high degree of intimacy. It is
possible for a person, as we put it, "to get himself across to
others". It is also possible for him to "be got across to", if
I may phrase it in that way. That is to say, there is an
openness, a sharing of relationship, a give-and-take, in
those who are personal which is not found, in anything
like the same degree, in that which is impersonal or quasi-
personal. It is sometimes pathetic to see a dog of whom one
is fond (and notice how one tends to use "whom" here, for
reasons which will be apparent shortly) attempting to

communicate with oneself. But somehow it can never quite come off, however much one may wish for it and however pathetic the poor dog's efforts to "get himself across" may be. Alas, one's beloved dog is not personal, however much he may have adumbrations of personality in his makeup. But *I* am personal although my personality may not amount to very much. With my family and my friends, my neighbours and associates, with any other man, I can communicate in this personal fashion, both giving and receiving. That double meaning of communication is predicable of God, in the highest or supreme degree. Not only can he disclose himself to me and affect me; he can also be affected by that which I do towards him. He is not only the supremely causative agency, shall we say; he is also the supremely affective one. What that last statement implies for our doctrine of God needs and will receive further development.

Furthermore, personality means some sort of genuine freedom. The word "freedom" is commonly used to mean ability to do whatever one happens to wish. But that is a very cheap and superficial way of regarding it. Genuine freedom has limits; these are set by the conditions with which one is confronted, on the one hand, and the sort of being one is, on the other. To be free means to be able to think and do, under the given circumstances, that which it is in one's nature to think and do. This is why "stone walls do not a prison make". The prisoner is *not* free to get out of his cell; but under the circumstances which are his, he *is* free to be himself as a man, to think his thoughts, to desire what he desires and love what he loves, and to hold to his manhood despite the most appalling attacks made upon it. (I know about "conditioning" and "brain-washing", etc.; but these have for their purpose the

annihilation of personality and over them, perhaps, a man
can exercise no control; yet they are not "normal" elements in the human condition.) In respect of God, too, we
can speak of his freedom – his freedom to do what is possible under the conditions which his creation has imposed
upon him, and his freedom to be himself in doing it. This
suggests at once that there are limits set upon God. Yet
even St. Thomas saw this, in his insistence on God's
inability to do that which contradicts his own nature; and
if we take the fact of the creation with sufficient seriousness, this means surely that by his own decision to create
God has set conditions of a creaturely sort that limit his
freedom to act. To say otherwise is to turn God's
"sovereign rule" (his being what the creeds call *pantocrator*)
into a kind of sheer "almightiness" which is irrational
and absurd and contradicted by our limited knowledge of
how things are in the world.

To be personal means also that one is either entirely
integrated or on the way to being so in a high degree. A
"split personality" is at odds within itself and lacks true
personal reality; that is why people who are in this state
are in need of medical or psychological treatment. None
of us, doubtless, can lay claim to complete integration, but
we are on the way towards it – or else we are losing our
personalism and on the way towards a less than human
existence. In God, we may say, integration is at its highest
– he is *all* God, everything centring in his self-awareness
and his purpose. Whatever may happen to him, as we
might put it, he can never be less than himself – he can
never be other than God, that is to say. And much may
happen to him, since he has the creaturely world to deal
with. From it he may receive an "amen" which opens up
for him new possibilities and novel opportunities of action,

3

or from it he may receive a "no" which denies him those particular possibilities and opportunities – in which case, we must suppose, he finds other ways, more subtle perhaps, in which his intended purpose may find its fulfilment. Again we may notice that temporality, of some sort, comes into the picture once more.

Finally – and this discussion makes no claim to be exhaustive; it is only meant to be suggestive – personality is marked by a capacity to love. Indeed I believe, for myself, that this capacity to love, and to *be* loved too (for loving is always mutual, always a giving-and-receiving, no matter what Nygren may say in his misguided motif-analysis in *Agape and Eros*), is the most distinctive quality of personality. As I shall argue in another book, love is commitment, mutuality (or giving-and-receiving), tenderness or persuasion, faithfulness, hope or "eager expectancy" (in von Hügel's splendid phrase), and desire for union. It is in these ways that love brings about the fulfilment which is personal in the fullest and finest sense of that word. Being personal, God is love. That is the best way in which we can define the divine reality; although if we said that God is Lover, and by this meant "cosmic" Lover, we should perhaps be closer to the truth. And since the capacity to love – and to be loved – is the distinctive quality of personality, it can be called God's root-attribute.

Now to say that is to deny, or at least call seriously into question, the whole trend of what Professor Charles Hartshorne has styled "classical theism". For that variety of theism has always insisted that God's "root-attribute" is *aseity*, or "being in and of and from itself". I began this chapter by disagreeing with that position; I still disagree with it. It rests back upon a false dilemma which philosophers and theologians have continually claimed to be

open to but two possible answers: *either* God is being itself,
utterly absolute, *or* he is entirely conditioned and relative.
But why should we be shut up to this choice? As Professor
Hartshorne has ably demonstrated in a whole series of
books, there is a third possibility: God may be absolute in
some respects and contingent or relative in others. And
that is exactly what the witness of Scripture, the heart of
Christianity in Jesus Christ, and the continuing experience
of believers would tell us, if only we listened to it with that
utmost seriousness for which I have pleaded.

Absolute, yes . . . but absolute in being (and here is
where the notion of *esse* comes in) always and utterly unsurpassable love, the unsurpassable cosmic Lover. Absolute . . . in his faithfulness; in the unfailing tenacity of his
loving purposes; his desire to be intimately related with
his creatures; his inexhaustible capacity to love and love
and love, and never to fail in his loving; his wisdom in
adaptation so that the best good in any and every situation
may be extracted and used for succeeding best goods. Conditioned, yes . . . conditioned in that he never violates nor
contradicts nor overrides the freedom of the creation, but
acts always in and under the creaturely conditions with
which, by his own previous working as well as by the response made in the creation, he is confronted. Relative,
yes . . . relative because he is always related to his world,
never withdrawn from it or in retreat to some private
heaven of his own; and because he is always affected by the
world, which makes a profound difference not only *to* him
(as if it were from the outside) but *in* him (because he
shares in, is participant of, and has involved himself with,
that world to the fullest conceivable extent). For God there
is no "out"; he is always "in" and "with". That, surely, is
what is meant by love, even on our own limited human

scale. And God's love is quite literally – although not in the conventional sense – infinite.

Young people these days have a strange language of their own. They speak of "being with it" and they talk of the places "where the action is". I venture to apply these phrases to God himself. God is always and unfailingly *with* his world – so much so that we cannot think of him apart from his world, and for this we have also biblical evidence since nowhere in Scripture is God talked about entirely "in himself" without regard for the creation where he is at work. And God is to be seen precisely "where the action is". What goes on has its derivation from his own activity, and in what goes on his creatures themselves are active; God moves in *those* places, not in some realm of his own where in supreme detachment he contemplates his own perfections. To say the latter would be to exchange the Bible for Aristotle; however many theologians have been willing to do this, no Christian in his moments of prayer and worship and obedient service has ever done it. This is why an Aquinas presents so puzzling a sight to our eyes; for there are really *two* Aquinases: the one who let Aristotle often subsitute for Scripture, the other who in his prayers and sermons and *explicationes* on the *Credo* and the *Pater Noster*, and above all in the *Corpus Christi* office, was entirely what nowadays would be called a "biblical theologian".

The God who acts in Jesus Christ is the living God. He is *living*, with a vitality and intensity of which we can have but the faintest glimpses. He is utterly *faithful* to his purpose, however much he may have to adapt himself to particular circumstances in order to accomplish it. He is unfailingly *loving*, not only in that he gives himself without reserve to his children but also in that he is "vulnerable" to what the creation does in its response to him. He is *in no sense impassible*, unless by this term we intend only that because he is inexhaustibly love with endless resources available to him in loving, he can never be defeated or overcome. And he is, in the most complete sense, *personal*: our personalities, as we call them, are faint reflections of his fulfilled personality. If that were all that was meant by *actus purus*, or fulfilled actuality, we could be content with the description; but alas, it is usually taken to imply that God is in no way affected by his world, and this we cannot for a moment accept since it denies everything that has been said up until now. More important, it denies the deepest insight of religious faith as Christians know it, even if many thinkers have insisted that no concept of God is viable which does not do precisely that.

When on occasion I have talked like this, somebody has often said, "Those are fighting words." Of course they are; but there *is* a fight going on here and the fight is about something of utmost importance to Christian faith – and indeed to all vital faith in the living God. That this is so may be demonstrated by a brief consideration of those who nowadays speak of "the death of God". What "god" is it, whose death they so confidently announce? If one examines their writings, it turns out that the "god" who is "dead" is the entirely transcendent, remote, miracle-mongering (in the worst sense of that word "miracle", a word which in our sixth chapter we shall try to save for its proper use), absolute, impassible, unrelational idol who has been substituted in so much conventional theology and preaching and writing for the *real* God who is living and active, giving and receiving, vulnerable yet inexhaustible, and "whose nature and whose name is Love". Some of these modern writers in fact are only atheists in the sense in which the early Christians were called "atheists"; that is, they are smashers of false idols. The tragedy of the situation is that for many of them the true God, active in self-disclosure in the Man Jesus, has never become a possible option, since the only conception of God they can entertain is of the other variety.

Several times we have spoken of temporality in relation to God. But, it will be said, is not that exactly what we cannot predicate of deity? The answer is, that it all depends upon what we mean by temporality. If the term is intended to describe *our* kind of successiveness, with its creaturely limitations to a partial retrospective-prospective mode of activity, then God is not temporal. But if temporality in God is understood as being a supreme mode of existence in the before-and-after, with all that is past ever present in the divine memory and all that is future open to him, so that genuine novelty is possible in the creation and the precise details of that novelty are not dictated in advance by God but (granted his awareness of relevant possibilities) can be new opportunities for him too; if that sort of thing is what is envisaged, to fail to predicate it of God is to fall back into exactly the same erroneous view of him as unaffected and unrelational which we have found reason to deny. As a matter of fact, within the main stream of "classical theism" there are already some indications of this kind of predication. For "eternity", applied to God, does not mean "timelessness" but "full possession of ever-lastingness" (Boethius' famous definition says just this). And if "everlastingness" or ongoing temporality is not denied in *fact* in such a view, then for God to know it, in the "simultaneity" of his awareness – in every "present", as we might say, if we do not fall into the *nunc stans* error which makes "every present" a single and unchanging moment without "befores" or "afters" – need not negate in him the kind of knowledge which leaves room for genuine contingency and unpredictability and which also allows us to think of God as himself sharing in that processive quality which "everlastingness" inevitably possesses.

What has been said so far in this chapter about God is, from one point of view, a series of variations on Whitehead's theme that "God is not the exception to metaphysical principles, to save them from collapse, but their chief exemplification". However, we have been making our start from the principles required to explain the meaning of "personal"; and we have been saying that God is "the chief exemplification" of *those* principles. As to the specifically metaphysical ones, if by this is intended (as is usually the case, although I should disagree with the procedure) that which is *abstractly* true of God as the necessary explanation of what is not God – that is, of the order of nature as a whole – we shall not discuss them in this book. I have written about them, elsewhere; and in any event, there is Schubert Ogden's admirable *The Reality of God* for the study of those who wish to pursue the matter further.

But what relevance does our discussion have for the questions with which we are chiefly concerned – with communion or fellowship, providence, "miracle", and prayer? It has a high relevance. *If* we think about these matters, we must think about them with some understanding of what we mean by God. The way in which we see man's communion with God will be determined very largely by how we think of God himself. So will the way in which we see God's "ordering" of events in a providential fashion; so will the way in which we think of his activity, general and special, and especially the great moments when more than at other times he seems to "come through to us"; and so will the way in which we envisage that most conscious and intentional contact with God which we designate as prayer. I shall not attempt, at every point of the discussion of these matters, to indicate the difference that is made by our taking the position, regarding the nature and activity of God himself, which this chapter has defended. The difference will probably be all too obvious for some readers. But spoken or unspoken, accepted or rejected, it will be there.

In the following chapter we must turn to the other side of the God-man relationship. There our problem will be about man himself. As I have said before, there are always two sides to any relationship; otherwise it is not a *relationship* but a merging into some amorphous and almost foggy identity. Hence we must talk about man. We have said a great deal about "Who God Is"; now we must try to come to grips with the question of "Who Man Is".

A NOTE ON THE USE OF HOLY SCRIPTURE

The reader may ask, quite legitimately, how Holy Scripture is being used in this chapter and elsewhere in this book. Let me attempt to answer this question very briefly.

I am not a fundamentalist; hence I cannot and do not appeal to the *letter* of Scripture. Neither am I one of those who simply dismisses the Bible as "another piece of religious literature". The Bible is the witness to a long-continuing experience of God's activity in the world and with men, as this was interpreted and understood by persons who with insight and dedication responded to what they took to be God's pressure upon them. Biblical images are the images natural to the people who lived in their particular periods; and these images were used by the writers to convey the meaning for them of that divine activity and pressure. Without some such images it would have been, as it still is, impossible to communicate at all.

What then is conveyed to us is a witness to God's activity, in a given and special area and during a given and special period of time; the witness is known by its being reported to us – how else could it be known? – and that reporting is through what we may style the biblical symbols, in all their remarkable variety yet with all their surprising unanimity in respect to *him towards whom* they point. Thus the biblical symbols are to be taken with *utmost* seriousness. They are not to be taken literally, for that would suppose that in and of themselves they are divine. Neither are they to be dismissed as merely incidental and irrelevant. They are to be taken for what they *are*. That is, for Christians they are indicative of something disclosed about God as he reveals himself to men; indeed, they are to be taken as telling us not only *something* about God but as telling *about God* himself.

So I am concerned to use Scripture in such a way that the main direction, the chief indicatives, of these symbols shall be used as crucial to our grasp of what God is; always remembering that because the "heart of Christianity is Jesus Christ" (as I repeat, almost *ad nauseam*), the fulfilment and completion, as well as the correction, of the biblical symbols is in that which God discloses of himself, and of man in relation to him, in the total concrete event which we describe by the proper name Jesus Christ. Thus in one sense, but that not the one conventional in these days of neo-biblicism, I write as a "biblical theologian".

A NOTE ON NATURE AND NATURE'S GOD

One gets a little wearied by the continued harping – by so-called "biblical theologians" and by so-called "radical theologians" – on the theme that God cannot be known through the world of nature but only in the world of history and human experience. It is irritation at this sort of repetitious, but never demonstrated, assertion that leads one to welcome so heartily another movement of thought in the theological world – a movement whose immediate provenance is North America but whose most popular expression may perhaps be found in the posthumously published writings of Pierre Teilhard de Chardin. I am referring to "process-theology", largely based on the writing of Alfred North Whitehead but now given a remarkable development by such theologians as Schubert M. Ogden, whose *The Reality of God* was published last winter by S.C.M. Press, and J. B. Cobb, Jr., whose *A Christian Natural Theology* came out in this country at the same time from Lutterworth Press.

One of the persistent emphases in "process-theology", important for the purpose of this book, is the insistence that in the natural world the working of God may be seen and something of his nature is revealed. As being myself a "process-theologian", now transplanted from the United States to the United Kingdom, I commend this type of Christian thinking to my friends on this side of the Atlantic. I believe it provides a needed corrective to much that is being said and written here and on the continent; furthermore, I believe that it provides an alternative possibility to those commonly offered us: an existentialist theology, a completely non-metaphysical theology, a theology using only biblical categories, and the older more conservative "confessional" or traditional theologies. If none of these four seems quite satisfactory – and many will agree that this is the case – perhaps a consideration of "process-theology" is in order. I think it is.

However, the purpose of this note is not to delineate the main points of such a theology, but to agree with it in its insistence on nature as a sphere of God's working and a partial revelation of God's purpose and character.

First of all, it is necessary to emphasise once again that the biblical narrative of "the creation" ("In the beginning God . . .", etc.), like other biblical material of the sort, must be understood "poetically". "In the beginning" does not mean "once upon a time" far back in history, when things got started; it is an affirmation that as a matter of principle, everything in heaven and on earth is tied in with and is the manifestation of the creative activity of God. When William Temple said that "God minus the world equals God; the world minus God equals nothing", he was getting at this point; although we might wish that he had been able to recognise that God without a world in which he is creatively active would be a God different from the God to whom the Bible gives witness – *that* God is so much the creator that for him *not* to be creating seems a contradiction in terms. However, the creation stories in Genesis are a way of saying that at the back of everything and in everything and as the explanation of everything, there is God's continuing creative activity. In *that* sense he is the beginning; and the old doctrine of *creatio ex nihilo* can be interpreted in *that* sense or in no meaningful sense at all. He is also the *end* of everything, for he is the One for whom the creation exists – and, for "process-theologians" anyway, is as much the supreme affect as he is the operative agent in creation.

By nature we commonly mean the realm of "sticks and stones", of primal dust, of inanimate matter, of animal life – in fact, of general evolutionary development up to man's historical existence and experience, although that too, very profoundly, is *part of nature*. I believe it is entirely incorrect to let ourselves think that the realm of nature, apart from man, is irrelevant to our understanding of God. The Bible does not talk that way; neither should we, however sophisticated may be our "biblical" theology. A considerable number of theologians appear to assume that because Jesus Christ, a man in history, is for our Christian faith the central revelation of God, it is only history with which we need concern ourselves. Thus we have writers saying that while of course *other* religions find God in nature – which usually, and erroneously, is described as purely circular or repetitive in character – the Jewish-Christian faith finds him only in the historical events in which men are involved.

What these writers forget is that history has a geography. Every historical event takes place *somewhere*, and that somewhere is the natural order. We cannot hope properly to understand an occurrence in what we call history if we do not allow for its location in the world of things. It ought to be obvious to us, unless we are wearing some sort of theological dark glasses, that the historical achievement of, shall we say, Pericles, was "conditioned" by the place where he lived, the forces of nature which had to be dealt with, the climate, the Greek sea, and much else that was *there* in the realm of nature. So too with the ancient Jews, as the Old Testament plainly records; so too in the days of Jesus and in the reception of him by the first Christians. And so too with us today as we respond to whatever of God's activity we feel to be brought to bear upon us and in us.

The fact is that both history and the men who make it are organic with nature. They are tied in with it and part of it. It is not only that man is composed of chemical elements and biological cells and the like. Man is also the product of nature, who has emerged out of long evolutionary travail through the ages; he is not oddly inserted into the world as if he were a stranger from another realm. The second account of creation in Genesis tells us this in a pictorial fashion when it says that God made us out of "the dust of the earth", which was then animated by God's "breathing" upon it to make a living creature who could have fellowship with his creator.

I have mentioned Pierre Teilhard de Chardin; he was one of the great exponents of the line which I have just been taking. He refused to see man as separated from the ongoing evolutionary movement; in fact, for him man was to be understood as the "end-product" of that movement, throwing light upon what it was all about. And for Teilhard, man was now given the duty of working with the process, as a "fellow worker" (or as Whitehead once said, "a co-creator") with God, towards the fullest realisation of all nature's potentialities.

We must not tear man away from nature; what we ought to do is to see nature itself in an historical – that is, in a processive – way. It is not merely repetition, nor is it only the reshuffling of a collection of particles of matter in interesting new patterns. It is historical because it is a realm in which new things have happened and are happening and will happen. It is evolutionary; and it includes the emergence or appearance of genuinely new things. As Pringle-Pattison put it long ago, we are confronted with "continuity of process with the emergence of genuine novelty". As such, the natural order discloses something about the God who is its principle of explanation, the One who is active in and through it.

Let me mention three things about God which we can learn from the natural order. But let me preface these by warning that this revelation is not a disclosure of God under his "proper name" of "loving heavenly Father". What we see in nature is not God "plain", so to speak. For Christian faith, at any rate, if man is to see God "plain" it must be under the incognito of manhood, which is why Christians believe that God is incarnate, en-manned, in the human life of the Man Jesus. We do not see God "plain" in nature, but we see something of what he does and how he does it, under *that* natural incognito. And from what he does and how he does it, we learn something of what he *is*.

The first thing I mention is God's *boundless creativity*. Like an artist, God is a maker; but as with the artist, his making is not automatic or mechanical, as if he were an artisan. It is richly imaginative, strangely lovely; in brief, it is aesthetic. Nature is beautiful. Of course there is the problem of evil – "nature, red in tooth and claw, with ravin" – but that is another subject and suitable for further treatment in another book. All I wish to insist upon now is that nature discloses to us a continuing creative drive or urge, appealing to our imagination and awakening our appreciation, and often wonderfully beautiful. A Japanese once said that since Fujiyama is so beautiful, whatever made it must be even more beautiful. An aesthetic glory, an imagination, creative dreaming and working, are disclosed in the world of nature. God is the great Artist.

Second, I suggest once again that nature reveals God as *faithful*. The scientist would put this by telling us that the natural order has an impressive regularity, so that one can count on it. Hydrogen and oxygen in a certain combina-

tion will always together be H_2O; we do not expect that
one day they will be $NaCl_2$. Patterns of behaviour, a
remarkable consistency, predictable regularity: these are
what we see in nature; and it is these which give stability
not only to scientific enquiry but to our human existence.
If *anything* could happen in the natural order, we should be
able to live only from hand to mouth. But because the sun
"rises" every morning and "sets" every evening, we can
make plans. Seed-time and harvest, summer and winter,
sunshine and rain, day and night . . . these are the symbols of that predictable regularity and consistency. The
creative activity in and behind them all is faithful; and the
"bow in the clouds" in the Genesis story of the Flood is the
biblical way of telling us that truth about God.

Thirdly, I should repeat my insistence that nature discloses a God who *does new things*. He does them, not by
contradicting or overturning or rejecting the old; evolutionary study shows that he does them by working subtly
and mysteriously so that out of the old comes the new.
There are always the consistency and regularity (God's
faithfulness); there is also the new, like the appearance of
man in the world of nature or (as Christians would assert)
the appearance of Christ in the world of men. All is tied
together in the faithfulness of God, but "there lives the
dearest freshness deep down things", in Gerard Manley
Hopkins' lovely phrase; and now and again that freshness
springs forth with remarkable force and lo! something
new has happened. "Behold, I will do a new thing," the
prophet Isaiah has God say (Isa. 43.19). The God who is
disclosed in nature is the God who does such new things.

God is creative in his aesthetic making, he is faithful, he
brings new things to pass: these truths, I believe, we can
learn if we look seriously and steadily and humbly at the

world of nature. The same God who discloses himself "in divers portions" in the order of nature also manifests himself in Jesus Christ. For it is that Word "by whom all things were made", as the prologue of the Fourth Gospel tells us, who shone through the life of Jesus, the Man in whom he was supremely and decisively manifest for us men "and for our salvation" (our authentic living). If ever God acted, it was in that Man. But we do God no service if we fail to remember that the same Word spoken in Jesus was spoken by the God who "in the beginning . . . created the heaven and the earth" (Gen. 1.1).

CHAPTER THREE

Who Man Is

Let it be noticed, at once, that the title of this chapter, like the title of the preceding one, has "who" not "what" to introduce it. This will make it clear that with man, as with God, we are speaking of personal being, with all that this will imply, and not of some sort of "stuff" which is manhood. Indeed we might say that it is almost improper, really, to talk about human *nature* at all, since this may immediately suggest that there is some possibility of discussing man, and men, in large general terms which would be appropriate to purely "objective" entities; whereas, with man, with men, we are having to do with all the intimate pathos – in the Kierkegaardian phrase – of subjective existence.

If there is any one thing that we have learned from contemporary existentialism, it is that we simply cannot think of other men, much less ourselves, in such supposedly objective terms. Man is one who commits himself, is "engaged", as Sartre puts it; and so soon as we recognise this, we have made it impossible for us to think of him without giving the most serious attention to what it *feels like* to be a man. Sometimes theologians have described man as if they were engaged in the dissection of some specimen in a laboratory. Much of what they have got

4

down on their paper-picture may be true enough, but the
difficulty is that they are talking about a corpse, not a man.
The specimen has been killed dead by their description.
The dynamism, which is integral to each and every one of
us, has been destroyed; and what is left is only a shell,
interesting perhaps but not very relevant to our discussion.

In the last chapter we have been led to see that by God
we mean the living One, whose activity is unceasing and
whose faithfulness is unfailing. He is "pure unbounded
love", as Charles Wesley's hymn puts it; even more precisely, he is the divine Lover always in purposive action in
his world — and supremely in human life. Again, our clue
is found in Jesus Christ. It is in him that we find focused,
as in a burning centre, both the activity of God as Lover
and the responding activity of man as the one who responds, positively or negatively, to that Lover. In Jesus,
we know, the response is entirely positive; in the rest of us,
alas, it is all too often negative. If God is personal in the
highest conceivable degree, man is on the way to becoming
personal; yet by his free decision he may, and a good deal
of the time does, decline to proceed along that way. In
consequence, by his negative response to the initiating love
which is God himself in action in his world, man elects to
become less personal than he might and could be. Yet at
the same time, the cosmic Lover will not let him go; renewed solicitations and invitations, often under very
strange and unexpected incognitos, surround him and seek
for his freely given "amen". And it is a legitimate consequence of Christian faith to be assured that in the end —
the long run, so to say, which may be a *very* long run; but
then God has all time to work in — every creature will be
held captive to the Lover-God. And he will be held captive by no coercive measures applied in thus securing his

acceptance, but by his own entirely glad and free response.

So then we turn to speak about man. We want to know "who he is", in the light of that heart of Christianity which is Jesus Christ.

Man is on the way to becoming a person, we have said. And we have already argued that to be personal means at least these things: to be aware and to be self-aware; to be purposive; to be free in choosing that purpose, within the limiting conditions of circumstance and the character of the agent; to be communicative and open both to giving and receiving; to be integrated or knit into wholeness; and to be able genuinely to love and be loved. All this is what it is to be alive, in the sense that *persons* are alive, with the dynamism which leads to and involves activity.

When a man looks into himself to find out what he *is*, he discovers that these elements are there. But he also discovers that they are not fully there; as we have indicated, man is "on the way", he has not "arrived". Thus we say that we are *becoming* personal, rather than that we *are* personal in the fully defined significance of that adjective. This "becoming" is of enormous importance when we seek to understand ourselves. And it is forgotten, often enough, by the diagrammatic sort of theological portrayal of "human nature". But to forget it, even to slight it, is to damage the understanding of ourselves, since we shall then be content with regarding man as definable apart from his relationships; and that will be absurd. Our dynamic, "becoming", quality is precisely *in* those relationships, with others and with God; without them we sink back into the amorphous and meaningless entity called "manhood", and then we are no longer ourselves in the warm and vivid reality which self-knowledge knows and delights in.

In several books I have attempted to provide a sketch

of the meaning of our manhood in the specific and personalising sense that we have just noted. Perhaps I may
refer particularly to *The Christian Understanding of Human
Nature* (Nisbet, 1964) – a title which I do not much like –
for those who would care to pursue in more detail the
approach which seems to me right. For our present purposes, however, a different way of attacking the problem
seems indicated. Here our interest is not so much in a
detailed analysis of the significance of our personalising
manhood in respect to all human relationships; it is in the
particular relationship which men may have with God
himself. *Vis-à-vis* the divine Lover, then, we must ask ourselves, "who is man?"

My first suggestion is that man is by creation an intended *lover*. By this I am seeking to point out that precisely as God is love-in-action – that is, the divine and
cosmic Lover – so man, who is God's creation, is made,
and being made, in the fashion which enables him to be a
creaturely or created lover. He too is to be love-in-action
on the scale and in the manner appropriate to a dependent
being. I am not happy with the use of the term "being"
here, since (as I have argued) man is best seen as on the
way to personhood; he is a "becoming" personality, so
that in the poet's phrase,

> "man is not yet
> But wholly hopes to be . . ."

However, the phrase "being" will serve if these qualifications are always kept in mind.

But to speak of man as God's "creation", who is "made
and being made", at once demands that we say something
about that status. "Dependence" has already been men-

tioned. This suggests to us that any proper grasp of our own manhood will require us to put the fullest stress on the contingency of human existence. We neither explain ourselves nor create ourselves, in any ultimate sense. It is true, as we shall see, that man is called to be a "co-creator" with God; but this is *with God*, not in independence of him. Hence even in his capacity to participate in the creative activity which goes on in the cosmos man is always in dependence upon the initiating and supporting "grace" of God – which is God's love-in-action in him, upon him, and with him.

Each of us depends upon many things. Our situation in the natural order, our place in historical development, our relationship with our fellow men, are all instances of this dependence which is unavoidable and must be accepted with proper humility. There is a kind of "cosmic impiety", to use a phrase once employed by Bertrand Russell, that claims for each man a remarkable *in*dependence in the world; yet nobody can really achieve this. The symbol of his dependence, as a finite creature, is death. Each of us *dies*; and each of us dies in his totality. Whatever may be said about the Christian hope of resurrection and eternal life, the patent fact is that we do die and that there is no Christian reason to think that there is some especially "spiritual" part of us ("the soul") which has a natural immortality so that it does not share in the death of our body. But if we die, then we dare not claim for ourselves the sort of independence which would follow if something or other about us was not the victim of that mortality. It is part of the genius of Hebrew thought to have seen this; it is one of the tragedies of Christian theology that too often it has been assumed that man is naturally immortal.

Not only is man a dependent creature; he is also an

embodied creature, in which whatever about him is rational or appreciative or moral is tied in with and a part of his corporeality. Gabriel Marcel once remarked that man does not *have* a body; he *is* a body. Common sense should have taught us this; the Christian faith ought to have made it plain to us. The enormous implications of our embodied status, without which we are not human at all, need not be pursued here; we must go on to note that this "body-ness" is also to be seen in our belonging to "the body corporate". Aristotle discerned that man is a "social animal". The Hebrew conception of "corporate person-ality", as some Old Testament scholars have styled it, leads to the same conclusion. And all that in these latter days we have learned about the way in which we are inter-related one with another, as the "cultural" or "social psychologists" are showing us, points in the same direc-tion. No man can live unto himself; in his embodiedness he is part of the total reality of manhood. Yet we should not think that this manhood is some ideal entity or even some vast thing-in-itself in which each of us happens to share. On the contrary, there is no manhood apart from particular men; and particular men, in their particu-larity, are the personal entities who participate in each other and by necessity live with one another and in one another. There is no such thing as an "impersonal man-hood", despite certain Anglican divines who used such a concept for their doctrine of Christ. All manhood is per-sonalised – that is, on the way to becoming personal; and precisely for this reason each man is participant in other men. To be personal *is* to be social, in the sense indicated.

Furthermore, man is equipped both physiologically and psychologically with the sexual instincts and drives which lead him to seek union with another of his own species.

Far too frequently this quite central element in our human nature has been overlooked in theological discussion. The result has been a portrayal of man which is eviscerated and lacking in the richness of the experienced fact of our manhood. Freud was not wrong when he focused attention on the *libido*, although it is often forgotten that in his later writings this *libido* was not simply genital but inclusive of the totality of man's striving. So also, when Plato insisted on the place of *eros* in human experience, he was indicating the inescapable fact that desire, which includes sexual expression, is not an incidental part of us but essential to us. The dynamism which is integral to the manhood of each of us is bigger than our strictly sexual drive; but it is not separated from that drive. The latter is the instrumental means through which the former realises itself in human action. Failure to see this will produce an attitude to our own existence that distorts and twists what are deeply rooted factors in our lives.

The words "distorts and twists" have just been used. These words help us to see another aspect of the "who man is" question. Not only is man created to be a lover; the horrible truth is that, having been and being so created, he is misdirected in his loving. Of course man as a lover is frustrated; that is not so much wrong as it is inevitable. Since we are finite creatures, and because that finitude imposes the limitations of circumstance and situation upon us, we *cannot* love in the fullest fashion – even in the fullest fashion which might in theory be possible for us. The latter is the case simply because whatever is said in theory, in actual *practice* the opportunities for loving are limited for every man. I have heard someone say, "I love the whole world." That certainly may have been his intention; but as a matter of concrete fact, he was deluding

himself. At best he could love this or that person or group
of persons. His intentions were frustrated by the fact of his
human limitations; and those limitations were produced
not by sin on his part but by the patent reality of all the
circumstances which locate a given man in a given place
and at a given time.

The "sinfulness" of man is not to be denied. But what
has been called "the sin-obsession" most certainly is to be
called in question.

The phrase "sin-obsession" was invented, I think, by
Percy Dearmer – about whom much has been written
lately because of the recent centenary of his birth. Whatever may have been the merits or demerits of Dearmer's
own discussion of the subject, I think that there can be no
doubt that a good deal of the reaction so widespread in all
parts of the world against conventional Christian ideas is
to be explained by a deep feeling that it is not only absurd
but positively unchristian to let sin be at the centre of the
whole of one's understanding of the Christian faith.

For example, anybody who reads Bonhoeffer's by now
celebrated protest against "religion", and reads it with
some awareness of the kind of Lutheran pietism in which
Bonhoeffer was trained, with its centring of Christian
experience in the fact of man's sinfulness, must see that a
very important, if not the only, element against which the
great German Christian martyr was making his violent
protest was precisely this obsession with man's sin. I
myself have heard a young Lutheran saying that the pastor
of the church which he attended always spent the first
twenty minutes of his sermon making the congregation feel
depraved, evil, wicked, lost, because they were such sinners, and the next twenty minutes alleviating the state of
mind which had been induced by what went before. In

this way, he said cynically, the pastor was able to give himself a position of enormous importance, for it was *he* who could deliver his flock from the ghastly mental and emotional condition which he had also succeeded in creating in them.

But I am not concerned with whether or not Bonhoeffer, or my young Lutheran acquaintance, accurately represented typical Lutheran piety. What I *am* concerned with is the undoubted fact that the proportion of faith has been very seriously distorted by the way in which not only much traditional Christian teaching but the theological movement sometimes dubbed "neo-orthodoxy", sometimes "neo-confessionalism", and sometimes (and wrongly) "Barthianism", has seemed to place its emphasis on sin as the precondition of all true Christian understanding. This was illustrated for me by a story told by a layman whose pastor thought himself to be a faithful disciple of Reinhold Niebuhr – although, as one who has known Niebuhr and his thought reasonably well, I think that the distinguished American writer would have disowned his "disciple". The layman told me that every Sunday morning the pastor devoted almost his entire sermon to telling his congregation that *they* were miserable sinners, that the *world* was utterly vitiated by sin, that *all* human social relations were tainted in the same way, and that a true Christian must be pessimistic about the human lot in its every aspect. Then, at the end, he spoke for not more than a minute on God's extrication of man from this situation through Jesus Christ. He never enlarged on the assurances of the gospel as the New Testament presents them; he centred all his attention on that for which the gospel is supposed to be the remedy and cure.

Now as every one who reads the New Testament ought

to know, the truth is that whatever is said about man's sinful condition there, the emphasis is on *God's grace*. The gospel is not centred in the old Adam in whom, for St. Paul for example, man dies; it is centred in the new Adam in whom life is given. Despite one of G. K. Chesterton's typical paradoxes, the "good news" is not "original sin"; rather, it is the divine love in action for men. Again the Anglican liturgy, we are often told, is "soundly" Augustinian in its supposed "realism" about man's wickedness; our preaching, however, is "appallingly" Pelagian, since it assumes that we can be up and doing something about things. I doubt if this charge is fair, even if Niebuhr is its reported source. But there can be little question that if ever there were a liturgy which was pervaded by the "sin-obsession", it is ours. One has heard many attempts to get round this. For instance, it is said that while obviously for most of those who repeat the words, "the burden" of their own sins is *not* "intolerable", certainly the sins of men in general are or ought to be. Of course this is true. But it misses the point that *most* of the people who are in church cannot, or do not, make this wider reference. Hence the impression which they receive is that the Church spends most of its time telling them, and trying to make them feel, that (as a young man once put it in my hearing, in vulgar idiom) "we're nothing but a lot of 'stinkers' ".

The communion service, which ought to be filled with the joy of participation in the victorious life of the risen Lord, has for many the appearance of being a service of almost unmitigated gloom. A very devout laywoman once said to me, when she discovered that the eucharist was to be celebrated on a certain morning, that she was sorry she had come to church that day, since she felt that the communion was such a sad and morbid service, unlike mattins

(of all things!) which had a more cheerful quality! We
know perfectly well that the stress on penitence in the
eucharist is not true to the primitive and early Christian
attitude, any more than it is found in the ancient eastern
liturgies. Yet so often in our liturgical revision we insist
upon leaving *in* far too much of that element. People who
have been incorporated into the risen life of Christ have no
business spending their time at the eucharist informing
themselves and others of their unworthiness, their abiding
sinfulness, their wrongdoings, and the like. They ought to
be sharing in the joy of Christ's resurrection, his triumph
over all that is alien to God's loving and righteous will,
and his imparting to them the grace which will enable
them to be truly his people. But many of the revisions of
existing liturgies do not manage to suggest this, although
some of the relatively new ones have succeeded.

The reader of these words may very well assume that
my purpose is to urge a pre-world war sentimental optim-
ism, removing from the Christian faith all that realistically
portrays the error of man's ways and his need for divine
forgiveness and help. Nothing of the sort! It is not necessary to fly to the opposite extreme when one protests
against overmuch talk about sin and overmuch reference
to it in services which (like our own conventional Anglican
worship) reflect the excessive individualism and sin-
centredness of late medieval piety. It is the *proportion* of
faith, as this is reflected in our worship and our preaching,
which bothers this writer. We have got our priorities
wrong, so to say; we have been led to see things in the
wrong perspective. That is all.

Or almost all . . . for what is needed above all is a
revision in our notion of what is meant by sin. "We have
offended against thy holy laws. . . ." But *that* is really a way

of reverting to the position of the Pharisees whom Jesus condemned for a legalistic notion of man's obedience to God. Once we have let ourselves think of sin as violating a set of rules, we are on the way to losing the point of Christian faith altogether. Sin is *not*, for the New Testament, essentially breaking a law; far from it. It is damaging a relationship. It is ruining a friendship. It is acting and thinking and speaking in such a fashion that love is hurt. Rules, laws, codes, and the like may have some place in the Christian scheme; but it is not the central place, nor is it the place where the real meaning of our human sinfulness is shown up.

If once we could get *that* straight, we should be in a position to see that the way to restore man is not to condemn him for his wrongdoing – a wrongdoing which is obvious enough to any honest person – but rather to love him into goodness. That is how *God* acts, if the Christian gospel is true. If such is not the case, then the gospel is *not* true and we might as well give it up altogether and be honest about it. The fourth evangelist understood this when he had Jesus say that he was not "sent . . . into the world to condemn the world" (John 3.17). He came into the world to "save" it; and he "saved" it by loving men and women with the love which is nothing other than the divine charity "which moves the sun and the other stars". The writer of I John tells us that "we love because he *first* loved us" – *not* "we love *him*", despite the error in the Authorised Version's translation; "we love", in *all* our loving, as a response to a love which has come to us, been shown us, given us, shared with us.

That is how we are won from our *false* centring on self, which is what sin genuinely comes down to. And Jesus himself was prepared to use all sorts of analogies from com-

mon human experience to drive this point home. That is
part of the glory of the Incarnation, as we call it: that God
himself works in us and with us in a fashion not unlike,
indeed very much *like* (but with an *o altitudo*, or as theologians would say, in "an eminent manner"), the way in
which in human relations people are won to goodness by
being loved enough to get from them a response of love.

If *this* understanding of the matter were really accepted,
we should not be "obsessed" by our sin; we should be
joyful in our acceptance by the great cosmic Lover who is
God. And when we talked about our sinfulness, we should
not be thinking all the time of our failure to keep this or
that law, to obey this or that rule. Sin would not be doing
this or that specifically *wrong thing*. What we should be
thinking about is the way in which, as an old confessor of
mine once put it, "we have hurt God's heart of love". If
all this is denounced as approaching close to antinomian-
ism, my reaction is "So what?" Christianity *is* antinomian
in one sense, since at its heart it knows but *one* law, the one
that the Epistle of St. James calls "the royal law" of love
(Jas. 2.8). In any event, I am myself prepared to say that
it is better to err on *that* side than to err on the other; it is
better to tend towards a quasi-antinomianism than to fall
victim to a narrowly legalistic piety. And I should argue
that Jesus himself made exactly that choice; which was
why the Pharisees condemned him but the "common
people heard him gladly" (Mark 12.37).

The meaning of human sinfulness, then, is not in man's
being man; it is to be found in his "distorting and twisting"
of his capacity to love. And for this he is himself responsible. Where there is no responsibility there is no sin in any
meaningful sense of the word. It has often been asserted
that man exists in a "state of sin"; and that is true. But the

"state" is not to be identified with man's finitude and the
limitations it imposes; to talk in that way is to fall into the
Manichean error of thinking the creation itself to be evil,
and no Christian can think that without denying the goodness of God in creating. "And, behold, it was very good"
(Gen. 1.31): the creation story in Genesis makes God say
this when he contemplates what he has "made". Nor can
any sense be made of the notion of some "cosmic sin" in
which we share. There may very well be evil elsewhere in
the universe; we do not have any reason to assume that
wrong choices, and the acts which follow, are limited to
human agency, and the biblical myth of "the fall of
Lucifer" may point to some wider extent of evil. But where
sin, in the proper sense, comes into the picture—at least
so far as our human understanding can go – is when and
as men have chosen to think and speak and act in a way
which violates the God-given intention that they shall love
in the right fashion. And the "state of sin" is but another
way of describing the cumulative effect of all the wrong
choices and consequent wrong doings of generations and
generations of human beings, who have thus brought
about a state of affairs in which we all of us must necessarily participate because we are indeed knit together in
one common and shared human existence.

Why do men elect to "distort and twist" their loving?
The answer to this question must be given in two parts.
First, we behave in this fashion (and by behaviour I
mean not merely outward acts but the total pattern of
manhood, which is always manhood-in-activity) because
we seek the immediate or short range satisfaction of our
strong desires. It is easier and simpler that way, as each of
us knows from his own experience. What is at hand is not
only more obviously available but also more obviously

attractive than some long range good which may be better for us. Second, because our wills are not perfect in strength, we are not able to put all requisite energy into our loving. Hence we are inclined to put even *less* than all our powers, limited as they may be, into our striving for the good available to us; in our acts of decision we are prepared to select the more readily attainable goals which we envisage as attractive.

In the last paragraph, I have been putting in another idiom the profound insight of St. Thomas Aquinas, who in the *Summa Theologica* analyses the problem with remarkable penetration and understanding. Our human difficulty is that we do not always *know* the best goods and that we *strive for* less than the best goods; it is also that even in our striving for the good, whatever it may be, we have succeeded by our own previous decisions in *so weakening our willing* that we are prepared to accept the second bests because we can at least reach *them*. But these things ought not to be, for men who are created to be personal and are therefore intended to be finite lovers of that which is the best.

But what is that "best"? Ultimately, it is God himself, who as love is the *summum bonum*. This is why even in his distorting and twisting of love, with all the frustration which limits and conditions it, man is *always* seeking God. He need not be consciously aware of this; in fact it would be preposterous to think that he is and psychologically absurd for him to attempt to be so all the time. But the *real* good, hidden under and working in every created good, is the goodness of God – it is his love which is there, evoking some response from his human children. This truth, upon which the main Christian tradition of moral theology has bravely insisted, is the explanation of such

astonishing statements as that which I like to quote from
Bruce Marshall's *The World the Flesh and Father Smith*: "The
man who rings the doorbell of a brothel is really seeking
God." In saying this, "Father Smith" was speaking with
the whole Christian moral tradition in its Catholic dress.
This does not imply that we should approve of "ringing the
doorbell of a brothel"; for doing that is precisely an
instance of the "distorting and twisting" upon which we
have laid stress. What it *does* imply is, first, that nothing
(literally *nothing*, if Aquinas is right, as I am sure he is) is
malum in se – evil in and of itself as a created entity; and
second, that what each man requires is to have his loving
rightly (Aquinas would have said, "proportionately" or
"ordinately") directed. When St. Augustine prayed, in
The Confessions, "Order my loving", he was saying just this.

Hence what is needed, if men are to realise in the right
meaning of that verb – that is, make come alive and real
and actual in them – their God-intended capacity to be
lovers, is an ordering of their loving which will be for their
own best good, as God's creatures living in community
with their fellows and fulfilling their true purpose. Yet any
serious analysis of self makes it clear that such an ordering
is not within the capacity of man. Of course he may *strive*
to order his loving aright; to a slight degree he may
succeed in doing so. But in the biggest and most complete
sense, this has to be "done for him". That, I am confident,
is the explanation of a simple yet frequently forgotten fact
of human experience; a fact which recent psychological
study, coupled with therapeutic measures whose effectiveness has been demonstrated by analysts and counsellors,
has confirmed. This fact is that "to love" we must *first* "be
loved". Many of the psychoanalytic experts would put it
in a different way, "to accept yourself and others you must

first know yourself to be accepted"; and Paul Tillich in *The Courage to Be* has used this way of phrasing it in order to help his readers grasp what is meant by the Christian doctrine of "justification by grace through faith". Yet it comes down to the same thing – that if anyone hopes to order his loving aright, he must know deeply within himself that he is loved by another. His response to that mastering love then enables him to proceed with the ordering; for it centres and integrates his whole existence in the other who is known to love *him*. When Andrew Chalmers wrote about "the expulsive power of a new affection" he was indicating this truth that when one is loved, one is released to love. But he might have gone on to say that when one is loved, one is also enabled to direct and pattern one's desires *towards* the initiating lover.

So we come to the place where we can speak meaningfully of redemption or reconciliation or atonement – whichever of these New Testament words we prefer to use to describe the putting of man on the road to his own true fulfilment, in community with his brethren, by the power (the love-in-action or the "grace") of God. There is *relationship* here; and this prepares us for the next chapter, in which "the relationship of God and man" will be discussed at length. For the moment, I wish to centre attention on the way in which "the heart of Christianity", which is Jesus Christ, illuminates the line of argument taken in the present chapter; or, it would have been better to say, the way in which that line of argument is derived from a serious confrontation with what is seen in Jesus Christ. We have insisted that Jesus Christ is not to be taken as if he were the *only* disclosure of God's will for man nor the *only* indication of the true nature of man himself. We are not to be "christo-centric" in that exclusive sense.

5

Yet what is seen in Jesus Christ is the confirmation and
coronation, the bringing to fulfilment, as well as the correction and implementation, of whatever else we may have
come to know about God and about man. We must avoid
the error of exclusive and dangerous concentration upon
the incarnate Lord which leads to the fallacy of "christo-
monism"; at the same time we must learn from Christ.

In Jesus Christ there is "perfect manhood"; so all the
classical formulations assert. But what do they intend by
that phrase? Certainly the primary significance of the
phrase is not found by calling our Lord "morally flawless"
or even "sinless". That was taken for granted. What was
intended was the full actualisation of whatever it means to
be a man. "Who man *is*", in the most profound meaning
of manhood, is nothing other than Jesus Christ himself.
Karl Barth has written brilliantly about this when he says
in his eassay on *Romans V* (a small pamphlet which was
originally an article in a theological journal), that while
chronologically the Second Adam (Christ) *follows* the
First Adam (man in his sin), ontologically the Second
Adam *precedes* the First. This is not quite exact, however;
for even chronologically, if we are talking of the mythological representation in Genesis, man was *first* in "original
righteousness". This is something all too often forgotten
by the "neo-orthodox" theologians of our day. While
Adam, "before the Fall" was not identical with Christ, if
by Christ we mean the Eternal Word of God or the
Second Hypostasis of the Blessed Triunity, as *man* he was so
much "in God's image" that his manhood was "perfect".
That is what he "fell" from. Yet Karl Barth's point remains true, with this qualification. If we wish to know
what *we* are, in the divine intention in our creation, we are
to look at Jesus Christ who is "perfect man".

What do we see when we look?

In the first place we see a Jew of the first century of our era. In his environment and with his historical background as a man, he shared in the life and thought natural to a man living at that time. His ways of thinking and doing, his attitudes and aptitudes, were those of a first-century Jew. Like every other man who has ever lived, he belonged to a particular place, at a particular time, under particular conditions, and with the limitations which all this imposed upon him. Even if Christian theologians have not been quick to recognise this, it is implied – necessitated even – by the common Christian conviction that Jesus Christ was *truly* man as well as "perfect man". The actualisation of human potentiality in him was not in contradiction of what we might style his "localised" manhood; it was precisely in and under those circumstances that it was actualised. There were the obvious physical characteristics of a Jew of that period; and there were also the psychological characteristics. To say otherwise is to fall into the Apollinarian heresy which supposed that the Eternal Word or Son *replaced* in Jesus his human mind. Furthermore, this means that he was limited, both physically or bodily and also psychologically. To give one illustration, Jesus' belief about demons was part of the furniture of belief in his own age; and the patent fact that he did accept such a belief and proceeded to act on it when he "cast out demons" need not demand that at a later time, when mental sickness is explained in another way, we must reject this modern assurance and insist that demon-possession is the Christian explanation of it – and also, because of who Jesus is believed by Christians to be, the true (because divine) explanation.

Granted all this, however, what do we see as the reality

of his "perfect manhood"? I suggest that we see three things; and that these are of absolute importance to us, not only in respect to Jesus himself but also in our concern with the God-man relationship in its integrity.

First, we see utter faith in God. By faith we mean here commitment, dedication, surrender – all that the existentialists have taught us about the "engagement" which establishes human existence in its subjective reality. Jesus was totally committed to God and to God's purposes; he dedicated himself to them with all his heart, soul, and mind; and he surrendered what might be styled "the direction of his life" to the God whose purpose he gave himself to fulfil. One of the ingredients of "perfect manhood", then, is such faith. Nor need we think that at every moment of his life Jesus was fully and vividly aware of what was the tenor as well as the *tendenz* or direction of his life. It is a matter of our human limitation, which Jesus shared, to attend at any given moment to this or that particular responsibility, this or that person, this or that action. What is central, however, is the underlying and undergirding commitment, dedication, and surrender; supporting and confirming the special moments of direct and self-conscious awareness. This we see in Jesus as the gospels portray him.

In the second place, we see utter obedience. In making such a commitment, in dedication with surrender, Jesus was intent upon "doing the will of him who sent" him. At point after point, when the temptation was strong to do something else, he recalled himself to the obedient performance of God's will for him as he had come to understand it. When in the Garden of Gethsemane he prayed, "not my will, but thine, be done" (Luke 22.42), we see no passive acquiescence in a terrible fate; we see the glad

acceptance, in complete obedience, of that which with all
his being he believed was God's plan. If this demanded
self-sacrifice to the point of death, so be it; "nevertheless
not my will, but thine, *be done*". I have emphasised the
last two words in order to indicate that this was an *active*
acceptance, with the intention that God's will *should* be
done, and that *he* was prepared and glad to be caught up
in the doing of it. He was "obedient unto death, even the
death of the cross" (Phil. 2.8). When (in Wesley's fine
words) "the sacrifice" was "made complete", it was
through precisely that willingness of Jesus to obey; and
through nothing else, for as St. Bernard once said, "Not
the death in itself, but the willingness of the One who died,
makes the sacrifice."

Thirdly, we see love-in-action. That is to say, we see
human love-in-action; and we who are his people see in and
under that human love the dynamic reality of the divine
love which is nothing other than the divine Lover. But it is
the human love that is immediately visible. "Having loved
his own that were in the world, he loved them unto the
end . . .", the end of loving them as utterly and completely as man can ever love, which is to say "to the point
of dying for those one loves". St. Paul understood and
stresses this. Towards God, too, we see in Jesus human
love-in-action. For what are faith, as he shows it, and
obedience, as he lives it, save the love which leads a man
to desire with all his being that the love of God work
through him? When in St. Paul's Cathedral, before the
Second World War, one saw the crucifix at the high altar
with the words *Sic Deus dilexit mundum,* one was deeply
moved at the profound insight of whoever it was who put
it there. Yet it was not only that *God* loved the world like
that; it was also that the *Man* "with his arms spread wide

upon the Cross" (as George Tyrrell once phrased it) loved
God like that – and in loving God like that, he also loved
men like that too.

I suggest, therefore, that "perfect manhood" as seen in
Jesus Christ is manhood totally given in faith to God,
entirely obedient to God's holy will, and penetrated by a
love which includes the world in its embrace while at the
same time it looks "up" (if we dare nowadays to speak in
such language!!) at the Father in equally loving regard.
None of us is Jesus Christ; yet Jesus is the full actualisation
of the potentiality in every man by virtue of his creation as
man and in the divine intention for him as man. If in our
"becoming" we are moving in *that* direction, then we are
on the right line of movement. If we are not moving that
way, then we are moving away from the goal which is
proper to us. In Whiteheadian terms, our "subjective
aim", to realise which will alone bring us entire "satisfaction", is to be found *that* way, in *that* direction. Hence when
we discuss the relationship between God and man, we are
to bear in mind that with all our imperfection and in all
our sin, the *truth* of "who we are" is there and nowhere else.

Such, I believe, is the result of taking with the most
complete seriousness the human side of that heart of
Christianity which is Jesus Christ our Lord and our
Brother.

CHAPTER FOUR

The Relationship between God and Man

The argument of the preceding chapters may be summed up in this way. *God* is the divine cosmic Lover, who is ceaselessly active in his world to create ever more occasions of good and who in respect to human life wills and works for the fulfilment of men as persons in community with their brethren. *Man* is created to be a lover, too, in all his finitude yet with all his capacity to give and receive in the mutuality which love signifies; it is in this way, and in this way only, that human life can find fulfilment. What is said about *both* God and man is said because in Jesus Christ, who is the heart of Christianity, the divine activity in the creation and in human life comes to its "implied goal and centre" (in a fine phrase of F. von Hügel); while human life itself is lived out by him in that fullness of faith, obedience, and love which are the manifestation of human fulfilment as God intends it and labours for it.

We have also said that Jesus Christ, as this focus of divine-human relationship, does not stand entirely and utterly alone – as if in him, and in no other place or time, God has "entered" his world to bring it so closely and intimately to himself. To say that would have been to fall

into the error which we have labelled "christo-monism".
Wherever men have responded to whatever they knew of
goodness, of truth, of righteousness, of beauty, of nobility,
there God has been at work, awakening that response and
evoking from his human children the best that they have
it in them to offer. In this sense we may follow those who
have been willing to speak of a more general and more
widely diffused "incarnation" or "incarnational action" in
a created order which itself is "incarnation" and "incarnational". If those two terms mean, as von Hügel among
others has suggested, "one thing working in another" (or
better, the cosmic Lover present and operative in all that
is not himself), the usage is entirely justified. So also is
the now frequently criticised notion that the world and
men are both of them "sacramental", a term which con-
veys the same idea. The denial of this position, simply
because its precise phrasing is not found in Holy Scripture,
is as unintelligent and absurd as other bits of biblicism,
whether they be fundamentalist or liberal. The word
homo-ousios is not found in Scripture; yet in A.D. 325 the
bishops and theologians of the Church, gathered at Nicaea
to combat the Arian heresy, were prepared to adopt that
Greek word as the only way available to them, in the
current philosophical idiom, for the safeguarding of the
essential biblical truth that in Jesus Christ very God, not
just a depotentiated half-divine even if supreme creature,
was present and at work as incarnate and reconciling. A
non-biblical *word* can express a very biblical *conviction*.

In such an incarnational world, Jesus Christ has appeared. In him God has brought to fulfilment that which
always and everywhere he is doing among men — namely
uniting them with himself so that they may become the
personal instruments of his love and find their own fulfil-

ment in that fact. Let it be noted that when the noun "instrument" was just employed it was preceded by the adjective "personal". This will make clear that God's "use" of men is not by pushing them about and treating them as if they were mannikins, without regard for their own freedom and integrity. The "use" that God makes of men is by their own glad and entirely free consent. Furthermore, men are so created that only when they are open to this "use" — I put this word each time in inverted commas to indicate that it is inadequate and may be misleading, yet it is the only one readily available for my purpose — are they truly and deeply *themselves*. The analogy here is to be found in human love and the response it evokes. "Your wish is my command," says the lover to his beloved; yet never is the lover so free, never so much himself, as when he sets himself to do, and freely wills to do, that which the beloved desires. Of this more will be said later, for it greatly assists us in understanding the God-man relationship with which this chapter is concerned.

We might put the argument, so far as we have carried it, by saying that in an incarnational or sacramental world, Jesus Christ is for Christian faith *the* Incarnation and *the* supreme Sacrament. As such, he completes and crowns what has gone before and goes on elsewhere; he also discloses the direction of God's working in the future. Furthermore, he corrects erroneous ways of thinking about God's nature and his operation, demonstrating both the error of those ways and also the truth which in their error they imply. He has "importance" (in a word much employed by Whitehead to signify some crucial disclosure of how things are) because he makes it possible to see what has already happened, what even now is happening, and what will happen in the future. He opens up new avenues of possibility for the divine-human relationship, through disclosing to men in act that which will bring them to their proper fulfilment. In the most profound sense he is *crucial*.

The concept of "importance" is so helpful in making this point that more must be said about it. Let us take an analogy from ordinary experience. Most of us know the triviality of daily life, where we do the usual things in the usual way, for weeks on end. It is all a matter of regular routine and we settle down into it, accepting what happens with equanimity. So it goes along, with our getting up in the morning, having our breakfast, going to office or shop or school, getting lunch, returning to work, taking the train back to our home for dinner, listening to the wireless or watching television, and then going to bed. Day in, day out, this is the routine. But that is not all that takes place in our lives. Perhaps we may meet someone who makes a tremendous impression upon us, perhaps we see a play which speaks directly to us, maybe we receive a telegram that tells us of the death of a person whom we have dearly loved . . . and this event, whatever it may be, alters the whole tenor of our lives. It is "important" to us.

Its importance is not only in the subjective effect which it has upon us, but also in the new possibilities it opens up to us. It throws light upon the past, it makes its impact upon us in the present, and it provides for us a new way of living in the future. In doing this, it has its objective aspect, for it discloses to us heights and depths in our own experience as well as unexpected hopes and desires for the days to come. It makes "a difference", as we say.

Now let us look at the history of this country. The ordinary affairs of state must be accepted; this government comes in and that government goes out; this budget is proposed and taxes are raised or lowered; things go on in a more or less normal and uniform way. But there comes a crisis, such as all Britons knew at the time of Dunkirk, or the sudden realisation of an economic emergency such as faced every subject of the Queen not too long ago. What does such a critical moment mean? It forces us to look back and consider what it was that brought us to this particular moment; it demands some immediate response to the exigency of the hour; and it opens to us, for good or for ill, new possibilities in the near and distant future. The event has been "important". Once again the quality of that moment is more than merely subjective. Something new *has* happened and we must make our adjustment to it. There is no escape for us, since the refusal to face the issue means that we have already acted upon it by default. Human history is made up of the ordinary routines and the exceptional moments, but it is the exceptional moments that give it its direction.

So far as we can see, something of the same sort is to be observed in the ongoing evolutionary process. There is the regular course of events; and then there is what biologists call a new emergent. The world of inanimate matter is going on its usual way; and then there is living matter. The world of living matter is there, behaving according to its regular pattern; and then there is a new sort of animal possessed of consciousness. The emergent changes everything. Something has happened and because it has happened things can never be the same again. Something new has appeared to alter circumstances. Often these "important" things seem almost infinitesimally small and quite insignificant; now and again they are very obvious and inescapable. But whether small or big, they have made a difference.

For the think ing man, recognition of moments whichare

"important" is necessary in his dealing with the facts. Failure to recognise them, when they appear, means that he is failing in his responsibility of participation in the general ongoing process in the universe as it impinges upon him. Professor Whitehead argued, particularly in his book *Modes of Thought*, that any adequate grasp of the nature of the world and the meaning of human existence must include an awareness of that which has this kind of "importance".

What he said has its relevance to man in his relationship with much more than the daily round, or the history of his country, or observation of the world of nature as he hears about this from those whose speciality it is. For the relationship of man with God also has its moments of "importance". When the Jews came to realise that God was concerned with the affairs of life, to the extent of making moral demands upon them, something "important" had happened in their national history. When the prophet Amos dared to say that God was interested in justice between men, it was "important". When Isaiah recognised that God could "raise up" a non-Jew, like Cyrus, to play his role in history, there was an "important" development in human relationship with that same God. Nor is this confined to the Jewish people. We may very well think that when a young Indian prince suddenly realised that one could not secure peace of mind and satisfaction of desire by continual striving, but only by inner discipline, an "important" point in human thought had been reached.

There is nothing impossible in the idea that among all the "important" moments in human history, insofar as man's relationship with God is concerned, one particular moment may have a very special "importance". And it is the Christian claim that precisely such a moment occurred in the total event which we call by the name of Jesus Christ. As we suggested a few paragraphs back, he is crucial in that relationship. So Christian faith claims – we believe rightly.

The relationship between God and man, understood in the light of this crucial concrete event of Jesus Christ as a fact in human history, is a free and open relationship. There is nothing coerced about it. When in the ancient Christian *Letter to Diognetus* we read the words, "Force is not God's way", we learn that in the earliest days of the faith this was understood perfectly well . . . alas, that it has been forgotten in later Christian thinking. God deals with us "as with sons", Hebrews tells us (12.7); we are not to think of ourselves as his slaves. In our attitude towards the God who is our heavenly Father, filial obedience is necessary; but that does not imply servitude.

God has made us to be free men; and in the truth which is given in Jesus Christ we *become* free. And that is both our human destiny and the truth of our manhood. It is obvious enough that in certain respects we are in the presence of "power", especially insofar as the natural order is concerned; there is not very much that we can do about hurricanes, tidal waves, and earthquakes, to mention only the unpleasant aspects of that order. But in the relationships where God permits us to know the intimacy of his ways in the world, where we are on our way to becoming personal, the situation is different. There response is secured by persuasive and not coercive means. It is a free response.

As I pointed out above, the right analogy here is human relationships. In his teaching, Jesus was always prepared to tell stories about human life and to draw lessons from

human behaviour. Sometimes such analogies are dangerous; but that is hardly to be regretted. Human life itself is
dangerous, which is why it is not entirely a matter of dull,
deadly, uniform complacency. Presumably God wants us
to be "up and doing", not to sink back in a kind of inane
lethargy; he has put us in a world where there is plenty of
risk. It is not surprising, therefore, that the analogies Jesus
used can be twisted and distorted so that they seem to
imperil the neat patterns preferred by conventional people.

In any event, very likely, Jesus' stories would imperil
such patterns, insofar as they are merely patterns of decent
conformity. As Whitehead noted, "love is a little oblivious
to morals" – especially the "morals" of the self-satisfied,
complacent, and conventional world. The life in freedom,
lived with God who is Love, is certain to put us into situations where risks must be taken. This suggests to us that
the relationship which we are to enjoy with God is a call
to adventure. Nobody can be entirely secure in such a
relationship. There is always an element of surprise, of
freshness, of the unexpected demand and the unexpected
succour. One does not wish to waste time in beating a
dead horse, but surely any Christian ought to see that the
relationship with God, exemplified for us in Jesus Christ,
is likely to be anything but humdrum; the "dead horse"
here is what our Marxist friends call "bourgeois respectability", and for most thoughtful people today it is indeed
a *very* dead beast. But it never was very much alive for
those who had caught a glimpse of the spontaneity and
delight of life with God.

I am not ignorant of the fact – it is too patent for anyone
to be ignorant of it – that much of what we see in Christian
circles reeks of that kind of respectability. This is not
because of an intrinsic connection between the Christian

life and the culture which for centuries has accompanied it. That relation of Christian life and culture has other explanations, with which cultural historians are quite familiar and about which they have written enormous and often unreadable tomes. There *is* one connection between the two, of course. This is the fact that what we might style the diffused effect of Christian faith, watered down and eviscerated, has created a certain kind of moralism which many of our contemporaries confuse with the genuine article, Christian morality. We can be grateful for the bits of Christian insight which from time to time appear in our culture; above all, we can be grateful for the sheer goodwill which men and women in that culture often manifest – although this is not unknown elsewhere, if we are to be honest about it. But it is certainly true to say, with Robert Louis Stevenson, that "respectability" (in the sense in which I have been using it) is "the deadliest gag and wet-blanket ever devised" for the suppression of "free men".

Once we have delivered ourselves from that all-too-popular confusion of conventionality and Christian life, we can go on to see that in the free and open relationship which men are intended to have with God – and which in Jesus Christ is established as a living reality into which we may enter – there is an enjoyment and happiness which redeems the inevitable moments of triviality. "The daily round, the common task" will always be with us, since the business of the world must be done. But they can be saved from *sheer* triviality by the joy which is also present for the man who lives with God. Once again the human analogy helps us. It is possible for a man who is deeply in love to do more than merely "put up with" the necessary routines of his daily life. He will delight in them, because they are being accepted for the sake of the beloved. This is not to say that being dutiful is the whole story. Despite Milton's famous line, to live as always "in the great Taskmaster's sight" is *not* the point of Christian existence. The talk about "Taskmaster" introduces into the God-man relationship quite the wrong set of ideas; it turns joy in freedom into bored acceptance of responsibility. The responsibility and the duty are certainly present; but God is not "Taskmaster", he is Love and a Lover, and the right approach to duty and responsibility is that which understands and accepts with a certain lightness of heart the tasks that are given. The tasks are not imposed upon us so much as they are evoked from us; hence we are glad that God has called us to be "fellow workers with him".

That phrase introduces us to the next element in the relationship between God and man. It may seem Pelagian to say so, but there is a co-operation between both parties to the relationship. Professor Whitehead, whom I am constantly quoting, once declared that we are made to be "co-creators with God"; that is not only a striking but a correct statement of the matter. If we are free men, who delight in doing God's work, we are also "come of age". God has treated us "like sons"; which in this connection means that he has entrusted to us, as a father to his sons, responsibilities and duties which will be valuable to him in the further working out of his purpose of good.

It is unfortunate that the words of Dietrich Bonhoeffer on this subject have been so much misunderstood, especially by those who dislike what he said. Sometimes it is thought that Bonhoeffer meant that we are *so* mature, *so* much "grown-up", that we have no further reason for bothering about God at all. But this is the last thing he meant; he intended quite the opposite. He was insisting, as the whole context of his remarks in his *Letters and Papers from Prison* clearly demonstrates, that because we are God's sons he commands us to act *like* sons — we are not to be the kind of little children who continually come running to our parents, asking them to do for us what we can do for ourselves and what we ought to do for ourselves if ever we are to grow up as true men. Yet in the totality of our relationship with God, running as a *leit-motif* through every thought and action, there is our co-operation with God in his great plan. Into that plan every detail of our existence can be fitted; it is all of it part of the pattern for good which throughout the cosmos God is working to achieve.

Here, however, we should be careful. Not every detail is *obviously* and at first glance a part of the great pattern. We have already spoken of the divine incognito; this doctrine is very much to the point here. A great deal of what each man does is carried out under the rubric: "Act, for God's sake, in this and that place, *etsi Deus non daretur.*" That was part of Bonhoeffer's insistence, let us recall: In the ordinary secular circumstances of life, he said, we must act *as if* God were not there; but we are to do this "before God", as he put it. We are to do it not only with the assurance that "underneath are the everlasting arms", but also with the conviction that in and through every situation and every task, God is present and working with us and for us . . . yet not "under his proper name", so to say.

It was William James, I believe, who once remarked that "God is no gentleman; he doesn't care what you *call* him." Sometimes he is called — that is, known and served as — love of friend or neighbour. Sometimes he is called justice for the underprivileged. Sometimes he is called truth, such as the scientist seeks to discover. Sometimes he is called beauty, which the artist and poet seek to depict.

6

Sometimes, and often, he is honesty and responsible service in business and school and industry and in daily con-
tacts with others. He may be called "taking care of little
Johnny, who is ill" or "nursing grandmother, who is
unable to look out for herself." My point is that in all
activity which is *right* activity, God is present; but he is
often present under his incognito and we are not to seek
to violate that incognito in those particular circumstances.

I have been arguing for what Paul Tillich called "the
autonomy of the theonomous". In every area of human
life, the proper observance of the "rules" must be part of
our response, and one of the rules is that God hides himself in order to make himself better known. The astronomer
will not find God at the other end of his telescope; La
Place told that to Napoleon when in the famous interview
(probably apocryphal) the Emperor asked if he had seen
God while engaging in his astronomical studies. Of course
he had not seen God; he had seen a star. Nor can God
be found at the other end of a microscope; Baron von
Hügel once objected to what he thought was Sir Oliver
Lodge's continuing hope to find God at that spot. God is
not known directly and immediately in such areas. What
is known are the "outskirts of his ways" in the world; and
since God is always *in* his "ways", being utterly *with* his
world, he is indeed known there, yet known by indirection
and by the fashion in which he makes things *go*.

There is no need to labour the point further. Let us now
speak of the more specifically *religious* channels through
which the God-man relationship is expressed. But before
we do that, it is necessary to say something about religion
itself, especially because in our own time there is a revul-
sion from thinking of Christian faith as "a religion" in any
sense.

This seems to me to be a beautiful instance of emptying the baby out with the bath-water. Certainly nobody should wish to deny that a good deal of what is commonly called "religion" has little if anything to do with Christian faith. I have already spoken, perhaps too shortly and contemptuously, about the perils of respectability. I must now note that ecclesiastical organisation, the whole paraphernalia of institutionalism, etc., – one could list here a whole catalogue – likewise has nothing essentially to do with Christian faith. This does not mean that *some* structures are not important, perhaps essential, to the continuation of the Christian reality as a living movement in the world. What it *does* mean is that church establishment, diocesan officialdom, parochial apparatus, and the bureaucracy that inevitably accompanies these, are accidental to those structures, not necessary to them in the particular *forms* in which such things are found today or at any other time. If this is what is meant by *religion*, then we must certainly agree that Christian faith needs to be distinguished from its husk.

Or again, the idea that to be Christian one must be a peculiar sort of man, with a particular fancy for what are styled "spiritual matters", is a denial of the genuine universality or catholicity of Christian faith and life. To think otherwise would be like saying that a taste for Bartok is an essential element in being human or, for that matter, in being musical. Some people simply cannot appreciate Bartok (I am not one of them, so I can use this illustration with impunity); but that does not suggest that they cannot be music-lovers and surely it does not mean that they are not human beings.

Furthermore, a very intense feeling of human sinfulness, especially of one's own, is not a condition for accepting the

Christian faith. That we *are* sinners is plain enough; and the contemplation of the love of God in Christ Jesus our Lord will shame any man into recognising that he does not measure up to *that* love, hence has fallen short of the proper reality of his manhood, and is therefore a "sinner" in the Christian meaning of that term. But not everybody can honestly sing or say words which demand that he shall have a devastating emotional awareness of his sin. Here traditional moral theology has carefully distinguished between contrition and attrition. The former is the recognition of shortcomings, failures, and sins, and the intention to do better in the future, all this in complete seriousness and with genuine earnestness. The latter is the internal disturbance, emotionally speaking, which for some people (doubtless because of their psycho-physiological makeup) accompanies that recognition – although often enough, a priest may say after considerable experience in hearing confessions, it can be an unconscious substitute for real contrition. Traditional moral theology, which makes this very important distinction, also asserts that what is requisite for pardon and absolution is the former or contrition, not the latter or attrition. We need not assume that to be a Christian one must have such a vivid sin-feeling – and if this is what is meant by *religion*, once again we must agree with those who condemn it.

So we could go on. But there is much more to religion than these things. Religion can mean, and probably in derivation from its Latin roots it does mean, the linking of man with God. In other words, it can mean precisely the "relationship" about which we are speaking in this chapter. In that case, it is indelibly associated with Christian faith, and every Christian man is *ipso facto* a religious man. Paul Tillich has greatly helped us in this matter by making another very important distinction between two meanings of religion which are often confused and hence confounded. Tillich has pointed out that in one sense, every human being has an "ultimate concern" with that which is "unconditioned". We need not enter here upon a sketch of Tillich's philosophical theology. Suffice it to say that he is indicating that every human being has something to which he is so related that it makes upon him absolute demands – and when we push this to its limit we can say that finally God is the "ultimate concern" of each man, although God may disguise himself in a great variety of ways in revealing his "ultimacy". Hence, in this first sense of religion, nobody can be an atheist; what he is atheistic about is some limited and limiting portrayal of "ultimate concern", which for one reason or another he feels compelled to reject.

In the second sense of religion, Tillich says, we have to do with particular practices, acts, beliefs, etc., which are how religion in the *first* sense traditionally and naturally clothes itself. In that case, religions may be better or worse, good or evil, true or false, helpful or harmful. In any event, religion in the second sense involves *ways* in which people are religious in the first sense.

Now from what we have already said, it is apparent that the Christian faith has to do with One who is taken to be "ultimate" in some meaningful (even if not necessarily traditional) fashion; hence it has to do with religion in the *first* sense. But it is also the fact that Christian faith embodies or clothes itself in acts and practices; hence it is also *a* religion in the *second* sense. I conclude that the current attacks on religion are the result of a good deal of mental confusion on the part of those who make them. What is required here is a little application of linguistic

analysis. What precisely is *meant*, what particular definition of the word is in view, when religion is thus attacked?
The end of the matter would seem to be that much of what
the critics dislike is what we also have seen good reason to
dislike, but that despite their rejection of the *word* "religion" they are often still very much devoted to the reality
of religion in its proper signification.

The specific acts or practices which as *a* religion Christianity has regarded as important to the God-man relationship may be briefly noted: personal prayer, worship and
sacrament, and action. About prayer we shall be writing
at length in the seventh chapter; hence we can move on at
once to the other two: worship and sacrament, and action.
Yet once again, a preliminary observation is demanded.
This has to do with what W. E. Hocking called the "worship and work" pattern. Every moment of every day cannot be spent in conscious prayer. Even in monasteries and
convents this is impossible, for the most rigorous contem-
platives have to eat and sleep. For the rest of us, the matter
is obvious. So too with worship and sacrament. Life is not
a perpetual church service (for which we may be grateful!); and the validity and importance of worship and
sacrament are not to be determined by the amount of
time, quantitatively speaking, we may spend at them.

A friend of mine once remarked that for him the whole
of life was a solemn high mass. One could only answer that
he needed to improve his notion of what the Catholic faith
was all about. For a solemn high mass, like all Christian
worship, is a moment (however necessary) in a total relationship; it may very well be the "high moment", but it
is not the only moment. There is an essential alternation
here – this is what Hocking meant. Worship and work,
work and worship . . . and I should wish to add, specific-

ally religious awareness and ordinary secular activity, if by "secular" we mean that aspect of experience where we do not consciously think about God but (as we have observed) serve him under one of his many incognitos in home, office, shop, school, studio, theatre, public house, or wherever else we may be engaged in doings which are not positively deleterious to our wholeness as men.

What is the significance of worship and sacrament in the cementing of the God-man relationship? I cannot do more than note some important elements or aspects of this significance.

The first of these is that all worship and sacramental act involve a two-way procedure. Because they are part of a relationship in which both members, God and man, are actively engaged – no passive affair, but a living reality – they imply doing on both sides. There is a movement from God to man; there is a movement from man to God. The prior movement, however, is from God to man; it is he who initiates and man who responds. This, we have seen, is nothing other than the paradigm followed throughout the theological declension of "God-world". God is first; he *always* is. Yet, as we have also seen, God in his initiating activity, called by theology his "prevenience" or "coming beforehand", does not *force* himself upon his children; he works to persuade them and to win from them their returning movement. That returning movement, therefore, is always free and uncoerced; it is the willing response made to God, who in his "lure" (as Whitehead put it) evokes from his children their own "amen". In this area, if in no other (I think there are *many* others) "the power of God is the worship he inspires". This is Whitehead again; and at no place, perhaps, is his deep insight more plainly demonstrated.

Second, the significance of worship is precisely in its cementing of a relationship which in any event exists. Worship does not bring God and man together for the first time; it establishes, deepens, makes vividly real, what is always the case. Even sacramental worship, in which there is a remarkable interchange between God and man, is not entirely unique; it has its adumbrations and earlier glimmerings in many primitive and less developed rites and ceremonies. These are exactly what St. Thomas Aquinas called them, "types and shadows" of the full-orbed Christian reality; but perhaps he was wrong in saying that they "have their ending" now that the Christian sacraments have come. It would have been better to say that they find their fulfilment and adequate expression in the Christian sacramental mode of relationship with God — maybe this *is* their "end", for "end" can mean, grammatically, either *stop* or *goal*.

Third, worship and sacrament are significant in that within the specifically Christian context, the mode of relationship which is realised — made real — is qualitatively different, although not entirely novel. The qualitative difference is found in the fact that they are "in Christ". The heart of Christianity is Jesus Christ; and he is both part of and decisive in man's relationship with God. He is part of it, because he appears in the setting which through the ages of the world and history has been prepared; he is no "bolt from the blue", but the expression of that which God is always "up to". On the other hand, he is decisive, because the relationship between God and man is in him intensified and deepened, to such a degree that it comes to what we sometimes call a difference in kind. I do not care for this way of phrasing it, however; this is why I spoke above in the words "qualitatively different". Karl Marx believed that quantitative differences could sometimes be so great that they became qualitative differences; this is part of his scheme of progression from one form of society to another. Whatever may be the case in such matters, it is certainly true that among men there is this kind of difference. And in the God-man relationship, we may claim, the difference may be found *a fortiori*.

If Jesus himself, as the bringing-together of God and man, is qualitatively different because of the decisive character of what God in act, and man in responding act, accomplished in the seamless robe which was his historical life, then the continuing relationship which was there established, and of which the Resurrection is the visible sign, is equally qualitative in its difference from other participation in the creaturely relationship with God. Furthermore, if Christian worship is a sharing in that relationship, in a focal manner, it too must be distinctive. Above all, the sacramental action of the Christian fellowship – where through the appointed means God in Christ and man in Christ are at one – must have its qualitative difference. Yet we should notice that this neither denies the continuities with earlier worship and with primitive and non-Christian "sacraments" – what R. R. Marett once styled "the sacraments of simple folk" – nor does it negate the reference found in all worship and sacrament to the common life of man in the world. This is what William Temple was driving at when, in words that have since become celebrated, he said that "one meal is called holy so that all meals may become holy". In another way of putting it, there are no absolute dichotomies here; but there are genuine and important differences. That is the way things are in this world of ours. Since that is the way they are, why (in Bishop Butler's famous aphorism) "should we wish them otherwise?" And why should we attempt, theologically or in any other way, to *make* them otherwise? We had better accept them "with natural piety", since there is nothing we can do to alter them. That is how God runs his world, for it is *his* world before it is ours.

For convenience, I shall discuss worship and sacrament together; and I shall describe the pattern of what goes on in sacramental worship. Other acts of worship are related to this, of course; but surely most of us will agree that the characteristic Christian worship is eucharistic. It is when and as we "make the continual remembrance" of Christ in the eucharistic action that we are most distinctively Christian, provided that we remember the action includes *both* the sacramental-aspect in its usual sense *and* the proclamation of the gospel of God's act in Jesus Christ. The eucharist is *both* Word and Holy Communion.

From God to man and from man to God, we have said. In the eucharist the pattern is quite plain, even if liturgical forms do not always manage to bring it out as clearly as one might wish.

There is "from God to man", first of all: God's giving of himself. This is found in the proclamation of the gospel, or the "preaching of the word", in which we are told about what God has already done and continues to do in Jesus Christ as the focus of all God's activity manward. But not only are we told; the word comes alive in the preaching, so that it is a present reality for those who hear it. In the specific sacramental aspect, the same giving is supremely exhibited. Here God in Christ "comes to us" through the instrumentality of bread and wine. Whatever happens *to* the "elements" — probably nothing, since any theory of change in the elements themselves would be a violation of God's ways of working in his world – the context in which they are placed makes a quite enormous difference. They are now the medium through which, under which, and by which Jesus Christ is brought to "dwell in our hearts by faith with thanksgiving". But to say "Jesus Christ" here is to say *God himself*. This is not because Jesus *is* God, which is the Monophysite heresy, but because in that manhood God acted in and with and through genuine human life to bring himself to us. It is also to say *man himself*, the pattern and power of true manhood now given to his disciples and friends as they "take and eat" and as they "drink this".

"From man to God" there is also giving. In this case it is response in faith to the proclamation of the word as preached. Above all, it is the offering of "ourselves, our souls and bodies, to be a reasonable, holy, and lively sacrifice" to God, so that we may be his faithful, obedient, and loving children. And there is even more, since we bring and give the tokens of the world's goods, as well as our own deficiencies "repented of", so that God in his turn may give them back to us for new uses and for the furthering of his purpose of goodness in the world.

Now all this is done "in Christ". Hence the early Fathers, not to mention John Calvin and Thomas Cranmer, were entirely right when they spoke of our being taken up "into heaven" and *there* by grace through the Holy Spirit "feeding on Christ". Of course heaven is not a *place*; Calvin and Cranmer were wrong in assuming that it was, although one can doubt if the early Fathers made *that* mistake. It is a state or condition in which God reigns in fully recognised fashion as the creative Lover. To be taken "into heaven", therefore, means to be given a proleptic share, an immediate yet eschatological participation (as modern theological jargon puts it), in the final fulfilment of God's purpose of good. It means also to be participant in the life of Jesus who is alive and regnant "with the Father", in some manner unknown to us, so that the eucharistic meeting with him is not a matter of historical reminiscence but a participation in the divine reality in all its eminent temporality. In Whiteheadian language, it is to be taken into and to share in "the divine memory", than which there could be nothing more real and nothing more enduring for any man.

All this must be referred back to our day-by-day life. Hence it is not inappropriate for the Latin mass to end, *Ite missa est*: Go, you are sent forth. From the eucharistic action – where the giving and receiving, receiving and giving in the faithful commitment of love, with all the mutuality and high expectation and the union of lover and beloved have been actualised both in principle and also through personal sharing in the life of Christ – the communicants go to their daily tasks. These tasks are part of the God-man relationship, too, and the Christian is to fulfil them with the delight in service which as we have seen delivers them from triviality and dullness.

The "going forth" brings us to our final topic in this chapter, Christian action as part of the relationship between God and man. About that topic I shall say only two or three things, very briefly.

First, action in the sense now intended is *always* "in Christ". That is what sacramental worship is all about; that is what Christian life "in the world", as we often put it, is all about too. We must remember, however, that when we say "in Christ" we are really saying "in Love". The first letter of that noun has been put in the upper-case, let us notice; this is because the Love to which we refer is nothing other than God himself. But it might also be in the lower-case, since we refer as well to the human condition of loving which is proper to man, however he may have "fallen" from it. Made to be lovers, we are to *be* lovers, now.

Second, Christian action has the same distinctive quality that Christian worship manifests. It is not absolutely discontinuous with other instances of human life; on the other hand, it is qualitatively different, since whatever is done is now done "in the Love" which was disclosed in act in Jesus Christ. This is its secret, which is to become an *open* secret, "in richest commonalty spread". As was said of the first Christian believers, men are "to take notice of us, that we have been with Jesus". Third, this will imply love-in-*action*, with courage and readiness to take risks, especially in a conventional society that values respectability above all else. It will imply *caring*, in the profound sense given that word by Baron von Hügel; or, in the fine Quaker phrase, it will mean "having a concern on our hearts" which will issue in deeds done for others. It will imply, above all, a self-forgetfulness in the service of the brethren. Thus our true selves will be found . . . and that is fulfilment in the most complete sense.

In the context of such a view of the relationship between God and man we can now venture to think about the specific questions of providence, "miracle", and prayer. Too often these questions are discussed *out of context*; hence they become purely theoretical or speculative, and sometimes they lack any vital meaning. The Christian way of looking at everything, in the light of that "heart of Christianity" to which so often we have referred, is an all-inclusive way. Christians ought not to pick at this or that problem, as if they were fretting first one bit of a large cloth and then another bit. In the States, some years ago, young people used to speak of "the big picture" when they wished to indicate that this or that detail could only make sense when there was a sound perspective on the matters which were at stake. So it is with the questions that shall now engage our attention. They must be approached in the context which the first half of this book has tried to present. Otherwise we shall not be able to come to any understanding of what our fathers in the faith were driving at when they insisted that they saw God's "hand" in what went on in nature and history; that they were conscious of moments when that hand seemed very plainly "laid bare"; and that they found their "native air" in communion with God in conscious and intentional opening of themselves to his never-failing presence. Nor shall we be able to commend these aspects of the perennial Christian way of thinking and living, unless we have always in our minds the setting for them with which in this chapter we have been so much concerned.

A NOTE ON CHRISTIAN FAITH AND MORAL PRINCIPLES

In recent years we have had a spate of books dealing with the problems of Christian ethics and with what in traditional terminology is called moral theology. Not only have subjects like war, racial relations, birth-control, labour-management problems, sexual behaviour in all its forms, etc. – been subjected to careful examination; we have also seen various attempts at a much more basic reconstruction of Christian morality itself, whether this be by an insistence on the contextual nature of ethical decision, or by the recognition of the situational aspect of morals, or by a reconception of the meaning of "natural moral law", or by some other device or method. On every hand we are told that the time has come for a very radical revision of the traditional moral pattern, sometimes (surprisingly enough) by those who might be thought to be defenders of that pattern. Here the work of some recent Roman Catholic writers comes to mind, as they seek for a way of restating, but with radical alteration, the Thomist position in respect to natural law but without following St. Thomas's own kind of application of that law to given instances.

The writer is not a professional *moral* theologian, but because he is a human being he cannot help being interested in moral questions; and because he is a theologian he cannot help feeling that the specifically theological background of all ethical discussion has sometimes been slighted by those with whose general view he is most deeply in sympathy. Or perhaps it would be better to say that he is convinced that *all* moral matters are basically *theological* matters.

To say that a man *ought* to act in this or that fashion is at the same time to say that the world is such that an action of the kind specified is in accordance with the way the world really *goes*. Otherwise, morality becomes nothing more than a catalogue of human preferences against the background or on the stage of a world which is supremely indifferent to man and his preferences. This is a possible position, of course; but it is worth observing that despite their disavowals of *any* religious faith and their espousal of a sort of theoretical atheism, men like the French novelist Albert Camus do not really succeed in alienating man from his universe quite as much as they think they do. For a documentation of this point, in respect to Camus himself and also to Jean-Paul Sartre, one may read with profit an admirable essay by S. M. Ogden on "The Strange Witness of Unbelief", included in his recently published *The Reality of God* (London, S.C.M. Press, 1967).

A truly viable morality, as Kant recognised, implies a general philosophical view; even more, it implies (as Kant was compelled to realise as he worked out his ethical position) what can be described as a theology – however inadequate or distorted that theology may be. And when a new slant is taken on moral issues, something also must happen to theological ideas. The converse is equally true. It is precisely here, as it seems to this writer, that much of the argument for a new view of the human situation, morally speaking, fails to recognise that a different theological position is the inevitable correlative.

Let me illustrate what I am attempting to say.

We are being told that love is the clue to the whole enterprise of man's moral existence. The morality of the Ten Commandments as "law" is often described as utterly irrelevant for us today; the value of such a code is seen only in the provision of a set of particular directives which help us to express love in the right way. Traditional ethical teaching is said to give us "guide-lines", which our ancestors found useful, in determining the way in which Christian love, which is the Spirit of Christ at work in men's hearts, can be operative in the world. What is not sufficiently understood is that a morality of code or commandment implied a conception of deity quite different from that which is implied in a morality of love-at-work-in-the-world.

It is true, of course, that some writers have been working in this direction. One thinks of the way in which the Bishop of Woolwich, in his booklet on *Christian Morality*, rested much of his case on the theological position that the deepest reality in the world is personal love. But he would not claim, for a moment, that he has worked out this position in any very adequate fashion. In Dr. Joseph Fletcher's *Situation Ethics* one does not find much theology; and its absence makes the book seem far too superficial and easy. The same cannot be said about Dr. Paul Lehmann's *Ethics in a Christian Context*, although one may wonder if the author has really followed through, *theologically*, his magnificent assertion that the divine will for man is to make him and keep him human. In other writing – one thinks for example of Dr. Paul Ramsey, with his rediscovery (if it may be called such) of "natural law" and his attempt to work this out in various specific areas – little awareness is found respecting the drastic *theological* revisions which are demanded. Dr. Ramsey's earlier "neighbour-love" or his more recent "agape-love" (with its various qualifications), and the new Roman Catholic insistence on "charity" as the basis for all moral discussion, must be given theological grounding if they are to be both intelligible and workable.

It is my own conviction that despite the disagreements about details, most of our contemporary moralists are clear that love *is* the key to our understanding of the moral dimension of life. But it is also my conviction that unless such moralists at the same time come to see that the conventional pictures of God's nature need to be changed, that key simply will not be possible for them to use.

We have observed that through much of Christian history, theologically speaking, the idea of God which has prevailed has been modelled after a self-existent and self-contained human life. God is indeed "love", but his root-attribute is his *aseity* – his utter self-sufficiency. With this has been coupled a view of deity that regards him as the great cosmic *law-giver*. He resembles some oriental

7

monarch, sitting on his throne, issuing edicts of one sort or another which his subjects must unfailingly obey. He gives "commandments"; he *speaks* and his word is *law*. He is not in any serious sense affected by what goes on in his world, despite the verbal assertion that he is a "loving heavenly Father" who cares for his creation. Of course I have exaggerated; and I have done it purposely in order to sharpen the contrast between a deity who essentially is himself without any necessity, of any kind, attaching to his relationship with his creatures. He creates entirely *ex nihilo* and he acts in the same way. If he is said to be *agape*, his kind of love is all giving without receiving; indeed some theologians have said that to speak of "desire" for a return on man's part is to reduce the quality of *God's* love to human *eros*, which *does* wish a return and is only happy when the return is given.

I regard all such ideas of God — whether as sheer unmoved mover, or *ens realissimum* (notice again the neuter gender of the Latin words), or as law-giver, or as omnipotent ruler who permits no "answering back", or as entirely self-sufficient in his aseity, as constituting in the last resort a denial of the basic Christian insight which is the consequence of taking with absolute seriousness the belief in Jesus as incarnate Lord. But that is not my point in this note. My point here is simply that none of these pictures of God, however traditionally hallowed, will permit us to think *morally* in the way in which we are now being invited to think by an increasing number of writers who insist on love as the basic meaning of Christian morality. There is a disjunction between the moral position that is being advocated and the theological position that is left, much of the time, entirely uncriticised.

A God who hands down laws is a God who is a law-giver.

Morality is then obeying those laws or suffering the consequences. A God who sets up a series of commandments is a God whose command is to be followed undeviatingly; to fail thus to follow is a violation of that God's explicit directions and is entirely unpermissible. On the other hand, a God whose nature is "pure unbounded love", in Wesley's glorious phrase, is a God who indeed wishes to make us human and keep us human, but does this by winning from his children a response which is itself loving. If we wish to have a morality that takes love as the clue to all human action which is genuinely human, then we must have a God who is himself essentially love and nothing else.

One may think that sometimes those who most urgently put forward the claim that love is the key do not themselves recognise that to say this is to say that the *universe* is directed by love; and that this means that ideas of punishment, retribution, penalty, etc., can no longer be entertained at all or (if there is value in them) need a most radical revision. For example, to think of God as the "judge" can no more be done after the analogy of the law-court; to talk of God's "justice" cannot be to talk as if, when he had tried love and found that it did not quite produce the expected results, he would impose another kind of requirement — rather like a father who having failed to win his children by persuasion produces "the big stick" with which to beat them.

I am not arguing for some sentimentalised theology, in which God is seen as benign and unexacting. If he *is* love, then his love can be terribly demanding, like all true love. It cannot be content with anything but the best possible under particular given circumstances. But it will *never* be arbitrary, nor will it ever give up its persuasive mode of working and resort to the coercion which contradicts its own loving nature. If we really believe that love is central to all morality, we must accept the consequences theologically. It is also, and equally, true that if once we believe theologically that the only adequate picture of God is sheer love, since this is "his nature and his name", then our morality will have to reflect what we believe. It is a tragedy that so much theology has not *really* thought this way at all; the result has been moralistic, in the pejorative sense, with an ethic which is so unattractive that one well understands why many reject it. But my main point here is the converse one: that a morality which is in terms of love entails a theology in the same terms.

This is not the place to attempt to work out all that is implied here. I have only the space to suggest that the position I have called "process-theology" does provide us, once we take it seriously, with a way of thinking about God as "pure unbounded love", in genuine loving relationship with his creation, affected by that creation and open to its response. This theology can give the newer moral emphases a theological context in which they make sense. Such a theology would grant a large place to human freedom, it would not regard men as "worms" but as lovers-in-the-making who are sadly frustrated and distorted in their loving, yet are open to the persuasive (loving) action of God in them and with them. It would involve tremendous modifications in our manner of talking about responsibility, judgement, consequences, and the like. It would help us to see sin as not so much violation of code as hurting of love. In fact, it would offer exactly the grounding which a morality of love requires if it is *not* to become sentimental.

CHAPTER FIVE

God's Providence in Human Life

In the chapters which have preceded this, we have portrayed the relationship between God and man, as this is illuminated by the event of Jesus Christ in whom we see, with singular vividness, "who God is" and "who man is". Now we turn to a consideration of providence – God's providence in human life.

Let us begin by observing that the word "providence", etymologically, signifies God's "seeing for us, and then making provision for, the way in which as men we must go". That way of phrasing it delivers us immediately from the idea that God *prescribes* for us in a predestinarian fashion exactly that which we shall do in the future, so that our supposed freedom is really an illusion and we are only passive puppets in the hands of a God who has already determined everything that shall happen to us. Such an idea would be a contradiction of what has been said already concerning God's dealing with us as free beings, in all the integrity of our manhood; it denies the basic Christian assertions concerning God's way of operating in his world, since it turns the world into some entirely mechanical apparatus which God controls as if he were operating a non-personal machine entirely subservient to his will and without any claim to a will and purpose of its

own. It must be confessed that some Christian theologians
have talked as if such were the case; yet in their own practice even these theologians have behaved in a fashion
which makes havoc of their theories. We must not fall
victim to those theories, however highly we may esteem
the men who held them.

Perhaps the best approach to the question of God's
providential activity in the world of men is by taking a
look at the well known and often repeated phrase in the
Thanksgiving Prayer in the service of holy communion in
the Book of Common Prayer. There we find that splendid
piece of English writing: "do all such good works as thou
hast prepared for us to walk in". As it stands, the phrasing
is somewhat quaint: to "do" what has been prepared for
us to "walk in" sounds odd to our modern ears. Yet the
quaint language points to an important truth to which we
ought to attend. And the way to get hold of the truth which
is there for us to grasp, is by looking once more at some
quite simple human analogies. As we have remarked on
an earlier occasion, we should have no fear of using these
human analogies; despite the obvious danger of pressing
them too far, we may remember to our comfort that Jesus
was prepared to use them. If he found them valuable, why
should *we* constantly draw back from using them? In this
particular instance, the human analogy is extremely helpful to us and we ought not to fear to employ it.

Let us consider, then, a loving father in his relationship
with his children. He is not a soft sentimentalist who has no
purposes of his own; on the contrary, he is a parent whose
sole desire is that his children shall grow to manhood as
entirely responsible yet absolutely free agents. He wishes
for them the best that they have it in them to be. Yet precisely because he is a *loving* father, he knows that he must

not coerce those children into any action which will be against their own understanding of the goal for which they must strive. He must not *drive* them; he must *win* them. Only in this fashion can they truly be themselves, not pale reflections of their parent. What does he do? how does he act?

The answer is plain enough, once we come to think about it. What he will do is to surround them with all sorts of incentives, invitations, solicitations, which will evoke from them their own glad response to him – not to his *ideas* about them, let us notice, but to *him*, their father. The way in which the father will set about this will differ, of course, from one child to another. Knowing his children and knowing each of them personally, he will realise that not every child can be treated in exactly the same fashion; he must adapt himself to the needs of the child, according to the capacities which he recognises as peculiarly *that* child's. In other words, each of his children will be thought of, each of them will be dealt with, as a person in the making. On the other hand, the father will not so vary his attitude and action from child to child that there will be occasion for one of them to feel neglected, or specially singled out from all the rest for good or for ill, or just plain eccentric. The children are *all* the father's children and must fit into and find their place in the family, understanding and respecting one another; but *each* child is also the father's child and he must be the father's child in his own right and with his own particular talents or deficiencies.

In thus dealing with his children, the father will provide opportunities for them to learn how to express themselves. He will give them his love, but he will not force that love upon them. He will provide occasions when they must act entirely on their own responsibility, making their own decisions and ready to take the consequences of those decisions. He will not "spoil" them, as we put it, by making everything easy for them, so that they have no obstacles of any sort to face and handle; if he did that, he would be wrongly protecting them from growing up to be truly mature personalities. When they are in trouble, he will be unfailingly available to them; yet even here he will not act in such a fashion that they fail to learn how to accept the "slings and arrows of outrageous fortune". One might go on with this account; but every parent will know what I am talking about, however much he may have to lament his failure to be that kind of parent.

This analogy helps us to come to grips with God's providential dealing with us. It is most certainly not a matter of helping lame dogs over stiles, neither is it a deliverance of men from the difficulties, worries, uncertainties, and ordinary problems of daily life. Those who have talked of God's providence in this fashion have had in their minds the picture of a father either so indulgent or so stupid that he did not, perhaps could not, recognise that men, if they are to be *men* and not mechanical toys for God to play with, must develop their own integrity and be free to suffer as well as to rejoice. Or such theologians think of God's children as such incredibly naïve and incompetent beings that one can only wonder what sort of idea they can have of the God who would create retarded children.

I now propose still another analogy; later we shall work out the suggestions that both of these analogies provide for delineating the providence of God the cosmic Lover. The second analogy is the relationship of a human lover to the man or woman whom he loves – a two-way relationship, mind you, just as the parent-child relationship is two-way and just as we have insisted that the God-man relationship must also be seen as two-way.

John has met Mary at a party. For his part, shall we say, he "falls in love at first sight". Mary likes him, but she has many other male friends with whom she enjoys going to the theatre, to dances, to dine in town. She is attracted to her new acquaintance, yet she feels that she must get to know him a good deal better before she is prepared to think of him in any serious fasion. What is John to do, if he hopes to win her love? He himself loves *her*, not just her pretty face or her shapely figure or her pleasant laugh. He is sufficiently intelligent to realise that one cannot *force* love from another person; hence he does not seize her by the hair and pull her to a cave where he can imitate his remote ancestors and by raping her *make* her love him. He knows that the result of such behaviour would be the contrary to the one he desires: she would hate him, not love him. Neither does he spend the time when he can be with her in nagging efforts to win her response. He knows that such acts would make her regard him as a bore, a bother, or at best someone to avoid as much as possible.

We all know what John will do. He will try to see her as much as he can, yet without obtruding himself where he is not wanted. He will do what he can to please her: if she likes chocolates, he will give her a box of them now and again; if she enjoys the theatre, he will arrange for them to see a good play from time to time; if she delights in dancing — and if he is not one of those who can only stumble about on the dance floor — he will take her to places where they can dance or invite her to some affair given by a club or society to which he belongs. He will be "nice to her", as we say; but this will not mean that in all their meetings he will be "sweetness" itself. Rather he will try to share her interests, understanding her likings, perhaps assist her in some work she has in hand. He will accommodate himself, so far as possible, to her interests and desires; yet he he will not let himself become nothing more than a carpet upon which she may walk, since he knows that no self-respecting girl wants to be a close friend of a man who has no self-respect himself. There may come a time when John will have to "go through fire and water" for Mary; but he will do it gladly – after all, he does genuinely *love* her.

Once again, it is not necessary to spell all this out in further detail. Every reader who has known love will understand the point. Furthermore, any friend who has genuinely cared for another, perhaps of his own sex, will grasp the significance of the analogy. So will husbands and wives, for it is clear that a married couple must be in something of the same sort of continuing relationship one with the other if their marriage is to be anything more than the provision of legalized opportunities for sexual intercourse or accepted occasions for controversy and quarrelling. Indeed, we may also say that much the same kind of relationship, perhaps at a less intense level, must characterise our day-to-day contact with our neighbours, our associates in business or shop, our schoolmates, and our colleagues. Less *intense*, of course; but not the less real. Otherwise human existence would be reduced to a series of minor, sometimes major, battles. And despite what the cynics say, human existence is not normally like that; it is not a continual state of armed conflict but a community of men and women who seek, so far as they are able, to "get along together" through exercising a considerable amount of what we call "give-and-take".

In other words, what I have been saying about parent

and child, about lover and beloved, about friends, about husband and wife, and about neighbourliness, has not been simply a matter of *ideal* existence. With all the necessary qualifications and all the honest recognition of failures *this* is what human existence is really like – as we know in our less pretentiously sophisticated moments. We are using for our first set of analogies *real* life, factual existence in all its concrete actuality.

Let us now look at the world itself, in which that existence is set. The greater portion of the time it seems to go on, as we might phrase it, in a fairly continuous and even stream. The Old Testament writer who spoke of "seed-time and harvest, and cold and heat, and summer and winter, and day and night" (Gen. 8.22) was describing what is well known to every man. There is a relatively predictable regularity in things; we can count on them and so make our plans with confidence that other things being equal they will not be ruined by some entirely unexpected exigency. This sort of regularity and predictability is the condition for such planning as is necessary for our own living; it is also the condition for the entire enterprise of scientific investigation and its consequences in the development of most of those technical instruments, household conveniences, and the like, which nowadays we take almost for granted, so accustomed have we become to them and so dependent are we upon them. But there is something more to be said about this relatively settled order. As a matter of fact, while it *is* indeed relatively settled, there are also the occasions when in a quite special way things happen which change the direction the world is taking, which open up remarkable new possibilities, and which have stupendous results in many different ways. Thus in addition to the regularities, there are times or points or instances of special intensification. Of these too we must take account.

But much the same can be said of what happens in our earlier analogies from specifically human activity. In these too there are the special moments. Not only does the parent continue with his child in the abiding relationship of loving care; there will come times, as each of us knows, when the parent must act in a very special way to meet a very special situation. So too with the lover in his relationship with the one whom he loves; there will be the moment – shall we say the *right* moment? – when he can perhaps dare to embrace her, or kiss her, or in less extreme ways indicate to her that she is in very truth the one to whom he wishes to dedicate his life. Likewise with married life; no marriage is *simply* the daily round of duties done, words spoken, tasks shared, although that is what constitutes a major part of it. There are also those times when marital love is expressed in more vivid and compelling ways. And in our friendships and our neighbourly associations the same is true.

If we take all these analogies with great seriousness, we shall not be surprised that in the God-world and God-man relationships there is much that is very similar. The most obvious point is the way in which we find the settled or relatively settled regularity of the relationship, on the one hand; and the moments, occasions, and places of more intensive expression of that relationship, on the other. To this we must return – it has to do with what theologians will call general and special providence, the resemblances between them as well as the distinctions which must be noted. But there is also the way in which the initiating or prevenient agent operates – religiously speaking, how God acts *towards* and *in* his world, how he acts *for* it as well.

Here our analogies are most helpful. But since we do not possess sufficient information to speak about that activity in its detailed operation in the world of nature – although there is enough for us to suggest that it is not totally unlike the activity which is known in our own experience – we shall concentrate our attention on that aspect of God's providence with which this chapter is concerned: his providence in *human* life.

First of all, God sets up the conditions under which we live. But we must not assume that he does this by some instantaneous act of creation. Surely by this time we are prepared to recognise that creation does not refer to some moment in the past, when with a "big bang" (my reference here is not to theories advanced by some astronomers in recent years but to the idea that once-upon-a-time everything came into existence) the entire creation was "made" and from then on has run like a machine. Creation has to do with an ongoing process, in which God "now and forever makes the earth and heaven", as Alfred Noyes put it in one of his poems. Furthermore, the process itself is a good deal more subtle than some have thought; it is a most delicate and intricate affair, in which by interpenetrative working new things are brought into existence out of what is already there to be "used". Perhaps the process of creation is a never-ending and also a never-beginning process; it is "always" going on. It may be recalled that even the Angelic Doctor found no reason, theologically and in abstract, to dismiss this as impossible; he maintained that creation was at a point in time only because in Holy Scripture, read by him in a more literalistic manner than would be possible today (although not quite as literalistic as some have thought – St. Thomas was no biblical fundamentalist), he believed that he found the assertion of such a temporal act or such an act in time. Creation as a theological doctrine has to do with the dependence of all that is not God upon God's activity, not with a particular moment in the past. And the ways in which that dependence may be envisaged are by no means prescribed – one may believe, for example, that not only is the world contingent in respect to God's action, but also that God himself is affected by the world in a degree and fashion quite different from the more traditional view which appears to think that his only serious relationship with the world is the logically necessary one of being its explanation. However these things may be, the point I am making is that God in the creative process does as a matter of fact set the conditions which make human existence a possibility.

Furthermore, in thus setting the conditions he establishes the circumstances that make human life not only possible but actually what it is. The regularities to which we have referred are part of this. Our whole environment, both natural and historical, is here involved as well. In the realm of the historical, God's manner of working is not identical with that in the realm of the inanimate in those areas, or better in those dimensions, with which physics and chemistry are concerned. There is a difference too from the strictly biological and physiological realm, although these also are part of the "conditioning" which makes human historical existence both possible and actual. It is all of a piece; there are no absolute dichotomies. Yet there are distinctions; and God's way in each dimension or area is the way appropriate to that particular aspect of the total creation.

It is obvious that if we were attempting a full-length study of the creative activity of God in the world, we should be obliged at this point to speak of what is called "the problem of evil". This problem impinges on human life in terrible ways with which we are all familiar. Yet in and of itself it does not make the providential activity of God in the world an impossibility for belief; it is a "problem" as well as a fact, which means that we have to do with certain particular moments or aspects in the world that are contradictory, or seem to be so, to the general run of things. This is certainly how a theist of any type must look at it; for the professed atheist, who has no prior belief in God as the agent of good, "evil" ought not to be a *problem* – it is simply another instance of the meaningless chaos with which he is confronted and he has no need to seek a "solution" for that, since by definition he is convinced that there *is* no solution available; it is all part of the absurdity of things as they are. I should like to refer the reader here to two excellent discussions which he may consult if he is unhappy with what may appear a too bland and easy dismissal of "the problem of evil": John Hick's *Evil and the Love of God* and Austin Farrer's *Love Almighty and Ills Unlimited*. These works are based upon the specifically Christian declaration of God as "Love", as the titles indicate; yet they take full account of the evolutionary way of seeing the world and they are insistent on the fact of evil, in its various dimensions, as well as on the horror of it – neither writer falls into the error of minimising it or explaining it away.

The course of human life then is played out in a world which sets certain conditions and provides certain circumstances for it. But there are also those moments or points or instances when in a special way God's providence is at work – this is, as we have seen, the aspect of providence which is called by theologians "special", as contrasted with the aspect called "general" to which the last few paragraphs have been devoted.

Now many people seem to think that special providence means intervention by God in his world in a fashion which delivers this or that person from dangers that confront him. We have mentioned Mr. Chesterton's attack on the "banana-skin" view of providence. Yet that view is very widely held. I believe that the best way of answering it is to quote at length from a now forgotten autobiographical essay by the great American theologian, Dr. William Porcher DuBose. Here is the passage, from *Turning Points in My Life* (New York, Longmans, 1911); it deserves our closest attention.

"Take for example, the truth of the divine providence: the old idea of 'special providences' was distinctly that even in natural events God acted outside and independently of a course of nature (or of an invariable natural sequence). We can no longer, shall not much longer be able to hold the truth of providence in that form. And yet I confess that I hold the truth of a universal and particular providence more firmly and I believe more really than I ever did before. I believe in a personal providence in nature, because I believe that nature is God, is how God acts and is in those things that we call natural because they are the operation of fixed and invariable laws. If those laws and operations were not fixed and invariable, we could not live and be rational and free in this world. Therefore God in natural things acts naturally and never contradicts or is inconsistent with himself. In so far then as his providence is in and through natural things, there is no deviation by any hair's breadth from the course of what we call the causation of nature. And yet, within the course of nature, if any Christian man will, as St. Paul says, love God and enter into the meaning and operation of his eternal and divine purpose, I know that he will find that literally all things are working together, that God is working all things together, for his individual and particular good . . . He never fails to help and govern those whom he brings up in his steadfast fear and love. I do not see where he promises to change natural things or natural sequences for us. I do see where he promises that in them all we shall be more than conquerors."

Very likely we should wish to rephrase portions of DuBose's argument. In view of our present knowledge of "nature" we should wish to allow for more of what has been styled "plasticity" in it; certainly quantum-physics and the principle of indeterminacy alter our way of speaking of "invariable natural sequence". Yet the main thrust of the quotation is clear; and DuBose's grand insistence on what is basic to the conviction that God acts providentially, both in a general and in a special way, is very important for us in our discussion.

What DuBose is telling us is that all talk of "special providence" must rest back upon a previous understanding of the relationship between God and man; this has been our own insistence, of course. Furthermore, he is asserting that what matters basically in God's providential activity is what happens to his children. In other words, God acts towards and in and for men to bring about that growing into personality of which we have spoken in our third chapter. If human life is a movement or a becoming, rather than a settled and finished product, then it is apparent that God's dealings with us will be towards bringing about the fulfilment which is the initial aim that he has given us and which by our own decision we have made our own subjective aim. We are being created in

8

such a fashion that we move in that direction, yet never without our own free consent. The fulfilment is to be achieved when the whole of our lives are centred or integrated in the love which God has for us and which we then, in our turn, manifest as a response. So "all things work together for good to them that love God . . ." and nothing, as St. Paul says in Romans 8, can finally "separate us from the love of God". But as St. Paul finishes the sentence, it is "the love of God, which is *in Christ Jesus our Lord*" which gives the peculiarly *Christian* slant to the conception of providence. This is not some vague benevolence, neither is it diffused goodwill; it is love made explicit in a human life which, precisely because it is human, we can grasp and be grasped by. There is no need to "climb up into the heavens" to find God; he is at hand, in the love of a Man who is our brother. Hence providence in its special sense is not some theoretical explanation of the odd coincidences with which life abounds, although it includes those coincidences; essentially it is God's doing whatever is necessary to bring us to him as love and to keep us there once we have let him take possession of our lives.

I have just spoken of "odd coincidences". Every man's life is full of them. There are the strange juxtapositions of this man and that place; the way in which we find ourselves confronted by the unusual challenge at a time when we least expected it; the chance meeting with the person who will turn out to be our wife or husband; the apparently accidental move from one job to another or from one house to another. These coincidental occurrences, as we call them, have contributed very largely to make us what we are — sometimes, it seems, for worse, and sometimes for better ends. Whichever it may be, here we are, at this moment and in this place. Now the peculiarity about a religious faith is that it is able to see in that whole mass of odd coincidences, set against the background of what might be called "the even tenor of life", a working of God as Love.

This was brought home to me very vividly many years ago during the period when I was teaching at a large theological college. It so happened that a distinguished clergyman had been asked to give a series of addresses during the two days which constituted the semi-annual "days of devotion". For reasons that were never disclosed, the speaker devoted all but one of his addresses to an analysis of the various reasons which brought men to offer themselves for ordination to the ministry. He spoke of the way in which some chance remark by a clergyman might have planted the seed; he mentioned that sometimes a choirboy was attracted to the ministry simply by being so often in church; he went further and pointed out how sometimes a young man who is an exhibitionist unconsciously chooses this vocation because it will give him an opportunity to "show off", perhaps in pretty clothes and very often in front of a large audience. He also spoke of the way in which persons who feel themselves inadequate to other walks of life can fall back on the ministry as an "escape from harsh reality".

On the whole, everything that he said was on the darker side. I do not know why he omitted other ways in which the notion of entering the ministry can come into a man's mind — such as admiration for some Christian leader, or desire to share with others in a very direct way beliefs which have come to be central to one's own life, or the simple wish to be of service to one's fellows. But this is not the matter under consideration. What the speaker was attempting, I suppose, was to show that in any man's life there is an enormous variety of psychological motivations and experiential encounters which may or may not lead him in this or that direction.

The last, very brief, address was an attempt to say that no matter what may have been each theological student's background, he could still consider himself a suitable person for holy orders if he would here and now honestly look at himself in the light of the task which the ministry imposes. He should have spent much more time on this positive aspect, but he did not do so. The result of this failure on the speaker's part was that several of us on the staff spent the next fortnight talking with the young men who came to see us, some of them in a panicky state of mind or emotionally much disturbed. The speaker had got through to them, certainly, in forcing them to analyse their own past as it bore upon their coming to theological school. I do not know, of course, what my colleagues said to the young men who visited them. For my part, the discussions went along this line: "Yes, such and such may have been the odd circumstance which first led you to think about entering the ministry. In and of itself, that circumstance is not determinative for you, or it ought not to be. Now that you know this about yourself, the question for you to ask is whether or not you *still* believe yourself a fit person for the priesthood, whether or not you feel that you have whatever talents and abilities are requisite, whether or not you can make the necessary promises at ordination, whether or not [and this was the crucial point] you are sure in your own heart that you want to keep to, and help others know, the Lord Jesus Christ, in whom God and man are brought together in an unparalleled way."

My own counsel was not adequate, but at least none of

the young men who talked with me decided to leave the
college; all of them, in fact, were later ordained and so far
as I know they are all admirable "servants of the servants
of God" in the priesthood of the Church. But for me this
little incident was a way of coming to understand three
things about the divine providence in the lives of men –
and I hasten to add that just because the men with whom
I was obliged to talk were future parsons, this does *not*
mean that what I am about to say is not applicable to any
and every man. Parsons are not "peculiar", in that sense
anyway.

In the first place, it became clear to me that providence in
its special sense is largely a *prospective* matter. It has to do with
what I have styled, following Whitehead, the "satisfaction
of subjective aim". Where am I going, in what direction
am I moving, how am I becoming a fulfilled personality?
– always remembering that to speak in this way entails
also the community of men to which by virtue of my particular personalising manhood I belong. Providence has
to do with vocation in the proper sense, which is the call to
every man to *become* a son of god "in Christ." Secondly, it
became clear to me that the odd coincidences with which
human life is filled are all *part of a wider pattern* which
brings us to the point of decision. Looking back over those
incidents, the young men of whom I have been speaking
might well have said: "God's providence was working
there and there, to bring me to do this or to avoid doing
that, to provide opportunities for me to move forward
towards fulfilment or in free rejection to fail to make such
a move." In that sense, the worse as well as the better
moments of a man's life can be "providential", provided
always that they are *used*.

There is a young man known to me (*not* a clergyman,

the reader will be glad to learn!) who went through school
utterly repelled by everything that he heard about "God
and all that stuff", as he phrased it when telling me the
story. He found the school chapel dull, save for the hymns;
sermons were either too theological for his schoolboy mind
or too "hearty" to earn his respect or too much concerned
with the sexual questionings of youth to provide more
than amusement. Sacred studies were dry and deadly in
their concentration on dates and names. The few masters
who were professedly Christian he either never knew well
or found repellent in their "official piety" – remember
that I am quoting his words now and again. He stopped
thinking of himself as a Christian. Then he came up to the
university. What had gone before had providentially prepared him – I dare to say this now, since it will now be
understood that the *prospective* reference is always necessary
when we speak of providence – to hear the authentic
Christian faith if ever he had the opportunity. By an accident, as it seemed, he went to the chapel of one college
where a very famous, not to say notorious, parson was to
preach; the sermon had to do with some matters which
were very deep in the young man's heart – his sense of
loneliness and frustration as a very fresh freshman in a very
large college of a very big university. He also heard some
lovely music in my own college chapel, again by accident
since his mother wished to hear the choir there and he
accompanied her. Finally, he was fortunate enough to
have an understanding supervisor who shared his tastes,
interests, and inclinations, and who was also a convinced
Christian.

Through the influence of that series of odd coincidences,
built upon the events of his past life at school but unex-
pectedly altering their significance, this young man be-

came, by his own decision, a professing and practising
Christian. But the fact that he did so brings me to speak of
the third thing I learned from my own experience in
counselling theological students. He, and they, had to
make a decision. In another way of saying it, an act of faith
or commitment was demanded before "the hand of God"
could be seen in the life of that man and those men, seen
(that is) in any serious sense. God can *only* be known in
that serious sense by a combination of decision and disclosure: decision on man's part, disclosure on God's. I am
indebted, of course, to I. T. Ramsey for those words; they
are admirable and with respect to providence they are
most enlightening. Our past experience, with all its odd
coincidences as well as its general trend, brings us to the
point. At that point we must freely choose. Then the future
is opened to us, where we have the assurance of the "Love
that will not let us go".

Divine providence and human activity, divine grace and
human freedom, divine preparation and human acceptance . . . this is the scheme. It is all in the setting of a
relationship between God and man which is given in the
fact of our creation; a specifically Christian stance is made
possible because of the double achievement of God in man
and man in God which is named Jesus Christ. The conclusion is that the Love which is nothing other than God
has led us in the past, through thick and thin, through
sorrow and joy, through danger and through ordinary
routines. That same Love invites each man, here and now,
to become a "fellow-worker" or "co-creator" by commit-
ting himself unreservedly to it and opening himself to
become its personalised instrument in the carrying out of
Love's purpose of good. And the same Love assures the
man who thus commits and opens himself that nothing

whatsoever can separate him from it. He may not always
be vividly aware of the supreme Lover; he may forget him
in the urgency of the job which must be done; he may, and
certainly he will, fail time and again and hence require
reinstatement and forgiveness so that he can start afresh.
Nevertheless, "the promise of God standeth sure." In one
of the New Testament documents (II Timothy 1.12)
which we call "Pauline", there are these words: "I know
whom I have believed, and am persuaded that he is able
to keep that which I have committed unto him . . ." *That*
is trust in God's providence, for it is trust in the God who
"provides" or takes care of his children. He does not re-
move difficulties nor save us from pain – he did not do
that in the case of his Son Jesus Christ. What he does offer
is the assurance of faith that enables each man to say,
"I am his, and he is mine, forever." Nothing other than
this, nothing less or more than this, is the meaning of
providence.

It is only when we set this enduring Christian conviction in the context of an enduring relationship between
God and man that it can be given any real meaning. For
us this means that it must also be set in the context of
whatever we happen to know, today, of the way in which
God works in his world – in other words, it must take into
account all that modern scientific discovery has revealed
to us of the patterns of regularity and consistency (the
reflections in creation of the divine faithfulness, as we have
noted), as well as the new occurrences which give freshness and delight to our experience. We cannot be naïve
about this, as if we lived in a pre-scientific age insofar as
our religious concerns were of importance to us. *That* kind
of alternation, in which we believe one thing on Sunday
and something entirely different the rest of the week, is an

impossibility for any of us who have intellectual integrity. And such intellectual integrity, surely, is a real part of our Christian faith too. To put it simply, God does not want us to be other than entirely honest men and women.

Mr. John Wren-Lewis and others have remarked that in one sense modern science is the most *Christian* thing that has happened in many centuries. It is Christian because it frees us to look at the world as creaturely and hence open to our investigation. Unlike some of our ancestors we are not obliged any longer to think that the world itself is *divine*; we are able to distinguish between the world and him who is present through and operative in the world. Science helps us to trace God's ways of working; but it does not reveal God in his proper nature as the divine Love which wills and works through the phenomena which science studies. Faith or commitment is required for that. All this is more than merely compatible with Christian thought; it is involved in it and a reflection of it.

With such an open mind towards that which we now know – and why should we take an attitude of *false* humility, as some advocate, and pretend that we do not know much that was unknown to those who went before us in the Christian faith? – we can yet talk meaningfully of the relationship between God and man and between God and his world. We can still speak of the providential way in which God cares for that world. But we dare not do this without always remembering that God's providence is but another way of speaking of his continuing relationship with his creatures. Providence *is* God's way of relationship; and it is only when the Christian affirmation of providence is firmly set within the context of the relationship between God and man that it makes any sense. But when it *is* set in that context it becomes a dominant motif in the life of the man of faith. It enables him to say, with St. Paul himself, as he looks ahead: "Thanks be to God, which giveth us the victory through our Lord Jesus Christ" (I Cor. 15.57).

CHAPTER SIX

The Religious Significance of "Miracle"

Probably there is no single aspect of traditional Christian thought which is so much under criticism, not to say vigorous attack, by non-Christians in our own time as the idea of "miracle". It is my own conviction that this criticism represents another instance of "birds coming home to roost", since no single aspect of Christian thought has been so badly misrepresented as has this same idea – misrepresented, that is, by many who have thought that they were defenders of Christianity

This may seem a very strange state of affairs; in fact it is. But if certain Christian apologists persist in presenting the idea of "miracle" in the fashion which so many of them have adopted, it is no wonder that they have not only sought to defend a hopeless cause but have also "given occasion to the enemies of the Lord to blaspheme". For what have these defenders often done? They have persisted in regarding the "miraculous" as implying inter-ferences by God in the natural order of the world, as "violations" of natural law, or (as is found in the more respectable self-appointed apologists) as a "suspension" of God's more normal ways of working. We shall discuss these ideas in succeeding pages; but it must be said at the outset that none of them is to be found in Holy Scripture – and it is precisely *there*, in the material which is found in the books of the Bible, that we are presented with accounts which involve the "miraculous". One would have thought that due attention to the specifically biblical understanding of these occurrences would have been a first charge upon defenders of Christian faith; alas, they seem to have preferred to centre their interests in non-biblical ideas and in doing so they have selected exactly the ideas which have little if any relationship with the main thrust of biblical thought.

It is certainly necessary, as we have argued, to employ non-biblical ways of regarding the world, a non-biblical conceptuality we might say, if we hope to preserve the integrity of the central biblical witness. But it is not necessary to select among possible non-biblical patterns those which have the effect of completely contradicting what the biblical symbols are intent upon affirming. We have seen already how such a practice has distorted the picture of God's nature and his manner of acting, so that instead of seeing God as the supreme Lover who intimately and unfailingly relates himself to the world and is himself affected by what goes on there, we are told that we must see him as "the unmoved mover", "the first cause", "being subsisting from itself", "the absolute", and all the rest of those images which only twist and damage the integral biblical conviction. We have seen also how this betrayal of the biblical material has created a whole nest of problems which never need have been there – not least in respect to providence, but equally unfortunate in respect to prayer, as the next chapter will attempt to demonstrate. As to the topic under discussion at the moment, the situation has become even worse. The marriage of Christian faith with a static philosophical theology has been disastrously unsuccessful; we see its result in the proliferation of "death of God" theologies, so-called, which are essentially a violent protest against all conceptions of God that make him a metaphysical monster. When we add the extraordinary "hang-over" of deistic notions of God in relationship to the creation which despite the defeat of deism in the eighteenth century still colour the thinking of many Christians, and not least many Christian theologians, we have a truly horrifying spectacle.

Indeed, so erroneous are the ideas conventionally associated with the very *word* "miracle" that one could wish – and to be honest, I do wish – that the word were given up altogether and the terms more generally employed in Scripture were substituted and regularly employed in all discussion of the matter. We shall speak of these terms very shortly. Yet it seems that this is too much to ask; hence we have placed the word "miracle" in inverted commas and we shall use it on occasion, not because it is a good word but because it is a familiar one and with all its mistaken associations might still be made to serve us, once we have engaged in a process of "disinfection", as one might say.

I turn now to the biblical material, in an effort to get to the genuinely Christian interest which is here at stake. For I am convinced that the *biblical* conception of "miracle" is absolutely essential to the whole Christian enterprise; and we must do everything possible to present that conception and show how it fits into and makes sense of the relationship with God and man which is disclosed in act, and made a possibility for others, in the life of Jesus Christ, "the heart of Christianity". What then is the intentionality, so to say, that we find in the various biblical stories of what are called "miraculous happenings" in the world and in human experience?

It must first be said, as plainly as possible, that in the Scriptures there is no notion of "natural law" or "the law of nature", in the sense in which these phrases have come to be used. This point has been made in Dr. H. H. Farmer's penetrating book *The World and God* – a book which discusses many of the topics with which we are concerned and gives special attention to our three main interests, providence, miracle, and prayer. But it did not require Dr. Farmer to tell us what ought to have been perfectly obvious to any careful reader of the Scriptures. It is of course true that the biblical writers knew quite as well as we do that there are enormous regularities in what goes on in the world and in history. They did not expect *anything* to happen. But their observation of the regularities, which they summed up when they spoke of the recurrence of "seedtime and harvest", "summer and winter", etc., was pervaded by a deep conviction which may be stated in simple words. "The faithfulness of God" was their most profound belief and they saw this faithfulness manifested in what we should call "the order" in the world. The story of the "bow in the cloud", given as a sign to Noah, is the most vivid biblical example of how they envisaged the regularities which they knew so well from their own experience and their observation of the world.

For them there was no impersonal natural order which once having been brought into existence continued without deviation. The whole conception of "secondary causes", as we have come to think of them through nearly two thousand years of philosophical and scientific enquiry, did not have any place in their understanding of the world.

It was *God* who was active in any and every event. Obviously this posed for them problems of a very serious sort. Was God the responsible author of all that was evil in the world? In one sense, yes, since it was *he* who acted in everything; and in some biblical material we find the attribution to God of "the evil that is done", although it is clear that in thus attributing it to him the writers were pained and puzzled. Later, however, the development of the idea of evil spirits or demons, under the suzerainty of the "prince of the devils" – a set of ideas which, whatever its background in specifically Jewish thought, was profoundly influenced by other eastern ideas, perhaps notably Iranian – enabled the biblical thinkers to relieve God of his immediate responsibility for the evil of which they were so conscious. Furthermore, they entertained the eschatological hope that in the "coming good times" God would overcome these evil powers and would establish himself as the sole ruler of his world. Even now, some of them believed (and here Christians emphasised strongly what for a few Jews had been perhaps no more than a pious belief), "the powers of the age to come" were *already* at work in this conquest of evil spirits.

We ourselves cannot accept this particular "theodicy", of course; but it may be that the insight of the biblical writers has something to teach us about the drag or pull "downward" (as we may put it in picture language) within a creation which is processive in its movement, under God, towards the fulfilment of his great purpose of love. However this may be, the point to be stressed is that for the scriptural thinkers and writers, the *regularities* in the world were explained by the faithfulness of God. Now this faithfulness, although it was undeviating, was also adaptable to varying conditions and circumstances. The Jews never doubted that men possessed some measure of freedom; nor do they seem to have questioned what must to them have been patent fact, that the world itself did not conform in its every detail to what God purposed for it. Yet God had the capacity, in his very faithfulness, so to work in the world that "even the wrath of man" could be "turned to his praise". And what was true regarding men was also true, in its appropriate measure, for everything else.

It is in this context that the Bible portrays for us those extraordinary occurrences in which God works with a peculiar intensity. I have put it in this way because it would be wrong, I think, to suggets that any biblical writer entertained the notion that God was ever "absent from his world" and hence had to "enter" it *de novo*, as it were. The language which is used in Scripture about God's "absence" (if this is the correct word) is descriptive of what my friend Professor Daniel Day Williams has called in another connection, "psychological absence". He was *felt by men* as being absent; yet it must also be noted that in that very sense of his "absence" there was also a realisation of his *presence*. It was to "test" or "try" his children's responsive faith in him and obedience to him, that God let them experience the dereliction which accompanied the lack of a vivid awareness of his being there with them in the events of their life. This, incidentally, helps us to understand how it may be said that on the Cross – in his "terrible dereliction" which led Jesus to cry "My God, my God, why hast thou forsaken me?" – it was still possible for Jesus to say "my God". With him too there was a presence in the very fact of felt absence.

In those extraordinary occurrences, recounted to us in the Scriptures, what do we discover? It will be convenient here to concentrate on the three New Testament Greek terms which are used to describe these, although Hebrew parallels can readily be found in the Old Testament. The words used are *semeion* or "sign"; *dunamis* or "power"; and *terrha* or "wonder". What do these terms mean, and what, in the light of their particular denotation, is their wider connotation?

A detailed examination would be more appropriate in a "word-study" than in such a book as this. Yet for our present purpose we can summarise fairly briefly the answer to these questions. A "sign" is the manifestation, in an actual concrete instance, of God's nature and purpose. The occurrence is meant to bring home, to this or that person or group of persons, who God is and what God is "up to" in respect to his human children. A "power" is the release of the divine energy, gracious as it always is, in this or that special situation, so that those present or affected by it can experience God's working and in consequence be strengthened and empowered more adequately to fulfil his intention for them. A "wonder" (and this is the closest to the conventional vulgar understanding of "miracle", yet with subtle differences) is an event which is so extraordinary and unexpected that it awakens awe and wonder in the beholder, making him say (as Professor A. E. Taylor once put it, in an admirable contemporary phrase), "Oh, my God!!" The "Oh" expresses the shock of wonder which the occurrence arouses; the "my God" expresses the realisation that in this happening, whatever it may be, it is *God* who is at work. This is no sheer "marvel", as if we saw a man walking in mid-air without visible means of support. Even in Latin, as St. Augustine pointed out, there is a difference between *mirum* or sheer marvel, and *miraculum* which in Christian thinking carried

9

with it (so the saint insisted) the recognition of *God's* hand at work.

Now what is to be noted is that in using these words it is not necessary to invoke any notion of divine interference in the world, as if God came into affairs for the first time or in an entirely unprecedented fashion. There is no necessary violation of any supposed "law of nature", neither is there any reason to think that whatever regularities there are in the ongoing of creation must be "suspended". We have spoken about "intensity" here; and that is perhaps the best approach that we may make to the reported incidents. God is everywhere and always at work; yet since he is personal in a degree and manner exceeding anything that we know, he can "intensify" his working in a given place, yet without contradicting or suspending or violating or interfering with the regularities which give a relatively settled ordering to the world.

Furthermore, it is to be observed that as in all instances of the relationship between God and his world, and a *fortiori* between God and men, there are two sides to be considered. The "mighty works" do not happen in a vacuum; they are not done nowhere and with reference to nobody. Failure to recognise this has led to a view of God as arbitrarily acting without context and without purpose, not to say without enduring result. "Miracles" do not just *happen*. They take place in a here, at a now, with certain persons present to observe them and to be affected by them. And to see them as being in truth God's working requires the faithful discernment of those who are on hand. A biblical "miracle" is not some magical performance by God for his own amusement; it is no sleight-of-hand trick designed simply to satisfy the divine sense of power. It is always for a purpose. The "mighty act" is to deliver the

oppressed Jews from their Egyptian pursuers; it is to
secure the life of a prophet whom God has sent to pro-
claim his message. In the New Testament it is to feed the
hungry, to heal the sick, to restore to mental stability the
emotionally disturbed, to awaken deeper faith in God's
loving purpose in Jesus Christ. And the consequence of
the happening, apprehended in faith as the very working
of God, is something in the lives of his children which gives
them new courage, new trust, new knowledge of his
gracious care for them.

So far we have been considering the biblical stories as
if they were all equal in their claim to historicity. But this
is an impossible position, as we all know. Hence there is
something more to be said; this has to do with the critical
study of the Scriptures, upon which for more than a century and a half devout Christian men have been engaged.
This can be touched on but briefly. The reader may consult any one or more of a vast number of books which sum
up the findings of this study, in all its different areas. And
it may be said in passing that one of the sad things in
current Christian circles is that the "assured results" of
this study have all too often been kept within the limits
either of the scholars' studies and classrooms or their
learned journals, or have been known very well to the
ordinary clergyman but not shared with the ordinary layman. Failure to make this material as widely known as
possible is the explanation of the bewilderment of lay
people when they hear of such newly discovered documents as the Dead Sea Scrolls and are quite unable to
relate what they learn about them to a wider context of
biblical enquiry. Much needless pain is caused thereby;
and for this, it must be admitted, the professional biblical
scholars and the parish clergy are largely to blame.

Biblical study has now made clear to us the extraordinary variety of material which is to be found within
the pages of the Scripture. It has taught us to distinguish
among these writings, recognising poetry where it is found,
prophetic exhortation, chronicle or annal (always given
us through the interpretative understanding of the writers
and dependent upon oral tradition as the precursor of the
written text), and the like. We have learned from it to take
account of the *sitz-im-leben* or concrete "life-situation" in
which the various books, or portions of books, had their
origin. We know about the comparisons necessary between
Jewish and later Christian ideas and their counterparts in
other religious traditions. Our knowledge is still growing;
he would be foolish who thought that we have now arrived
at absolutely secure conclusions about all the material
found in Scripture.

For our present purpose we need only say that a consequence of this vast accumulation of knowledge is the
necessity to examine each and every reported "miracle"
recorded or witnessed to in the Scriptures of both Old and
New Testament, in an effort to reach a sound and considered judgement as to whether it has a claim upon us as
being historical or whether it has some other significance in
the total picture. I shall not make a personal judgement
here, thereby saving the reader from pondering the question for himself in each instance. All that is necessary for us
is to say that there is a very high probability that many of
the stories are "written up", as the scholars put it, while
others seem to rest back upon a very likely incident which
was remembered and handed on to later generations. Our
interest in this chapter is not in the question of which, if
any, of the reported "signs" or "powers" or "wonders"
about which we read in the Bible may be taken as rela-

tively factual. Our interest is with the point of the "miraculous" in the life of the Christian believer today – in other words, it has to do with the manifestation of God's love, the release of God's power, and the awe-inspiring and wonderful expressions of God's care for his children, within the context of that continuing relationship between him and them to which so frequently we have been obliged to return. This is no affair for academic consideration only. It is at the heart of the whole Christian life.

Look through the history of the Church, for example, paying particular attention to the lives of some of the great saints. It so happens that just before writing this page, I was reading a recently written study of the various bits of historical and quasi-historical reminiscences of St. Francis of Assisi. Two things struck me with extraordinary force. The first was that Francis and those who wrote about him had a singularly naïve view of the particular details of God's way of working in the world. It could not have been otherwise, of course, for even if these simple men had been interested in the science of their time, such as it was, they would have been obliged to look at matters in a way which to us must seem incredible. This is just another way of saying that they, like every other man or woman who has ever lived, can only think about things in the terms available to them at a given time and in a given place. The second thing that struck me, however, was that despite this pre-scientific point of view, there was about Francis and his friends a quality which is absolutely central to Christian profession – the quality of trust in God's care for his human children, the readiness to see in that which happened to them signs of that care, and the most complete commitment of self to the God who thus loved his children.

This point – trust, capacity to find God's "hand" in his

works, and surrender to the reality of God working in his
world – is not dependent upon a particular scientific
world-view. Doubtless most of us would not be able to
look at our daily experience in just that naïve way which
was natural to Francis. On the other hand, something of the
same simplicity of life, with its openness and receptivity,
is possible for us. Something of the same awareness of the
divine at work in the natural and the human *is* for the
Christian in any age a part of his stance. *How* he will talk
about it will depend for him on the general pattern of
thought, the accepted scientific position, of his own time.
For Francis this pattern was not too far removed from that
of the biblical writers who gave us the stories about Jesus.
For us the pattern is very different indeed. Confronted by
what might have been the same set of events, we should
give a "scientific account" which would be as different as
is that general pattern of thought. And yet for a genuine
Christian theist God is *there*. As we said a few lines above,
this is not a matter important only for the scholar secluded
in his study; it is a matter of Christian "life and death".

What sort of world is this, in which we live?

For altogether too long, we have been the victims of
that deistic error to which reference has been made. Creation took place a long time ago, we think. Now the world
is going along, more or less "on its own", according to the
prescribed rules which God once upon a time laid down
for it. It can be explored by the human mind, with more
or less adequacy. We can control it in certain respects, so
that it will serve our purposes. But it is very much like a
great complicated machine which has been made in its
entirety and which runs on fairly satisfactorily, until a
moment comes when it needs repair or when some piece
of the intricate apparatus has to be replaced. Then its

Creator once again introduces himself. He tinkers here or there, he inserts the new piece, he makes the proper repairs; then off he goes to let the machine run on again in independence until there is another occasion of breakdown that requires another bit of intervention to set things right.

This kind of "cosmic-tinker" has aroused the ire of the Bishop of Woolwich and many other devout modern Christian thinkers. A "god" like that is a singularly undivine sort of deity, they think; and they are entirely correct in thinking so. A "god" who is simply "up there", with occasional visits "down here", is no deity for men to worship. In any event, there is no special reason for believing he exists at all. But the "god" who is "out there" is in equally bad case. Such a "god" exists for one purpose only: he is to provide a metaphysical explanation of why there is a world at all. But he is not intimately and directly involved in his world, nor does that world touch *him* in the heart of his being. He is a logical construction, good or bad as the validity of the argument may determine; but his relationship with his world is entirely one-sided. The creation is contingent and depends upon him, since after all he is its supposed explanation; but so far as he is concerned, the only relationship that he can have with the world, being an abstract metaphysical principle, is a logical one — that is to say, he is the end of a syllogistic argument. To such a deity we may do what Whitehead said we have done, namely "pay him metaphysical compliments"; it is hard to see how we can worship him with all our heart and soul and mind, love him, and know that he has from all time loved us too.

As earlier discussion in this book will have made plain, I am of the opinion that the philosophical orientation which is most suitable for Christian use is that commonly known as "process-thought". That orientation is at the poles from the one that I have just been describing – perhaps parodying. Far from being "up there" or "out there", God is right *here*. In Whitehead's words: "God is *in* the world, or nowhere, creating continually in us and around us. This creative principle is everywhere, in animate and so-called inanimate matter, in the ether, water, earth, human hearts. But this creation is a continuing process, and 'the process is itself the actuality', since no sooner do you arrive than you start on a fresh journey". (*Dialogues of Alfred North Whitehead*, by Lucien Price, p. 297).

God, thus understood, is no absentee deity; he is not one who having once created a world has now left it to itself. He is everywhere in it; or to put it more adequately, it is everywhere in him. This is "panentheism", to be very sharply distinguished from *pantheism*. The latter identifies the world and God; the former distinguishes clearly between them, yet does not find it necessary for that distinction to make a total separation between the two. Admittedly some seem unable to see the difference between *separation* and *distinction*; yet a Christian theologian should have no difficulty here, since his familiarity with the Chalcedonian definition of the person of Christ should have taught him that the Fathers of the Church, expressing the meaning of Christ in terms available to them, made precisely this point. In Christ, they said, the two "natures" of God and man were "distinct" but they were *not* "separate". The whole point of orthodoxy in respect to Christ is to insist on this: distinct yet not separate. What I should now wish to claim is that this point, which is classically asserted about Jesus Christ, is also in its own fashion true of the whole cosmos as it is related to God. The world is *not* God, nor is God the world; yet the world and God are never separated, although always and everywhere they are distinct one from the other. This is why in an earlier chapter it was possible to say that the world is "sacramental" and that God is ceaselessly at work in that world "incarnationally". It is also why it was possible to affirm that the event of Jesus Christ, as the bringing-together of God and man, is both continuous with all of God's working in his creation yet also focal within that working and hence marked by the distinctive quality to which I made such frequent reference and upon which I so strongly insisted.

When Cardinal Bérulle made his striking statement that "the Incarnation is the manner and mode" of all God's working in the creation, he had in mind the single event of Jesus Christ. But there is no reason why that aphorism may not be given wider application. If we confine it to *the* Incarnation, we are in grave danger of mechanising that event, as well as isolating the Lord Jesus from the world in which he appeared and lived in our manhood. If we see *the* Incarnation not as a *confining* of God's action in the world but as a *defining* of its "manner and mode" we are liberated to make our own those great words of G. M. Hopkins,

"The world is charged with the grandeur of God.
It will flame out, like shining from shook foil."

Further, it is now possible to give a fresh significance to the familiar position that God is both immanent and transcendent. He is immanent, in that he is ceaselessly present and operative in the creation; and because the creation is open to him by the very fact of its *being* his creation, he is "becoming incarnate" in it, to greater or less degree, until in that one place and at that one time his "incarnating" achieves its fulfilment in *the* Incarnation. I have said "achieves" to make clear that God is doing something here; the living God is active in his world. The "achievement" is not dependent for its accomplishment simply on the fact that one man at that point was willing to open himself to God in that manner, although this is certainly part of the truth unless we deny to Jesus' manhood any genuine integrity and freedom. But the initiating, prevenient, preparatory activity is God's, who has "prepared and made ready the way" for that "fullness of the times", in his lure (as Whitehead would say) inviting and evoking response. What is more, if we do not confine our thinking about the Incarnation to the discrete person Jesus (of course no man *is* thus discrete, as we have sought to show) but include the preparatory movement which went before it, the response which was made to it, and the results which followed it, we can see that our Lady is part of the picture too. When she said, as Luke's gospel reports, "Be it unto me according to thy word" (1.38), she was in very truth "the consenting cause" of the Incarnation of God in Jesus Christ. Traditional Catholic theology has always said this, in spite of criticisms and attacks upon it; but that theology has not seen all that is implied in saying it. We have just noted the further significance of the saying of it; and that significance is the way in which we can guarantee both the divine initiative and the human response, not only in Jesus Christ himself but in everything that made his life among us a possibility.

Immanent and incarnating . . . and also transcendent. The perspective we have adopted makes it possible to speak of transcendence without falling into the error of spatialising the concept. Transcendence now means something much grander and more compelling of worship; it means the utter inexhaustibility of the divine love, which is adequate to handle any and every situation without losing its integrity or changing its purpose. There is always "more" in God than he employs in his particular activity in the creation; hence he is to be trusted as able to bring to bear upon each situation not only the immediately obvious energy of love which *we* see, but much more than we can even imagine. His "victory over sin, evil, and death", as it has been phrased, is assured; because he has at his disposal not only all the time there is, but also all the reserves of love that are his ineffable secret.

Thus to call God transcendent is not to indulge in just another of those "metaphysical compliments" which Whitehead deplored; it is to recognise precisely such integrity, faithfulness, and inexhaustibility as we have seen are in his very nature and way of working. It is this combination of immanence and incarnating with transcendence which calls forth from the human heart its adoration and worship. Worship is no cringing before an arbitrary tyrant, no fear in the thought of an absent ruler who at any time may thrust his power upon us. It is the "heart's submission" to him who truly is "worthful" – which is to say, unspeakably loving and inexhaustibly good, absolutely trustworthy because he is absolutely faithful.

With such a picture in our minds we can begin to make vital sense of the signs and powers and wonders which the word "miracle" is intended to suggest to us when we use it aright. It is very closely linked with God's providence, as should now be obvious. Perhaps we may even say that "miracle" *is* God's "special providence", *vis-à-vis* men.

Such a suggestion was made many years ago in a now forgotten little book by the late J. M. Thompson, one-time Dean of Divinity of Magdalen College, Oxford. Thompson was compelled by ecclesiastical pressure to give up the exercise of his ministry; he was regarded as an outstanding "heretic" because he was convinced, on critical grounds, that the "miracle" stories in the New Testament were so "written up" that it was impossible to think that they happened as reported. Yet he was equally sure that they pointed to something of enormous importance; and in *Through Fact to Faith* (lectures given at St. Margaret's, Westminster, as far back as 1912) he wrote these words: ". . . if the word 'miracle' be given up, what can we put in its place? There is a quite suitable alternative, the term 'Providence'. It is a good word, and has (on the whole) good associations. It expresses very well God's continuous and active care for the world; for we are misusing the term (and we know it) when we speak of God's Providence apart from God, or appeal to it as an arbitrary power external to our lives – as in Samuel Butler's satirical remark, 'As luck would have it, Providence was on my side.' We speak also . . . of 'special providences', meaning God's particular acts in the history of nations or in the lives of individuals; so that the term is well suited to express both the general and the particular aspects of God's activity. Further – and this is perhaps most important of all – the word suggests the regularity and permanence of God's work, together with the ideas of affection and forethought; it is a good antidote to the sense of something irregular and abnormal which is associated with the world 'miracle'." (*ibid* p. 48) Thompson then goes on to say that since all this is the case, in the remainder of his discussion of God's working in the world "we will therefore speak in future of the providential, not of the miraculous, action of God in the world".

I believe that Thompson showed great penetration in this suggestion and that we shall do well to follow his line. What this means in practice is that in those moments of our awareness of God's special presence, signifying his nature as love, as well as in those releases of his loving power in our own lives and in our awe and wonder at that which we see him to be "up to" in the world about us, we can take all of them to be signal instances of the never-failing providential care which he exercises in creation. They are no violations nor intrusions nor interferences nor suspensions; on the contrary, they are (as we may put it in popular language) "more of the same thing". They are those "intensifications" of which I have already spoken. They have about them the freshness which awakens in our own deep places a spontaneity of response; yet they are not thrust upon us entirely *de novo*. Or we may say that they are indeed *new*, but they are not cut off from what else we have known of God in our abiding relationship with him. It comes down, then, to another illustration of what we have styled continuity with qualitative distinctions.

It should be obvious that science is in no position to affirm or deny such experiences. The various scientific disciplines are concerned to describe so far as may be, and with as complete accuracy as is possible, the regularities in the several areas with which they have to do. The occurrences called "miracles" are not excluded from the realm of nature and history, of course; they do not take place in some trans-natural or trans-historical world, for so far as we are aware there is no such world at all. Precisely because the signs and releases of power and awe-awakening occurrences are part of a continuing relationship between God and men, they must take place in the world in which we find ourselves. And precisely because they are within the context of that relationship and occur within this world, they may very well be studied by the scientific man. He may or he may not be able to provide what some people like to call "a natural explanation" of them. If he does, the man of faith has nothing to fear, since the "natural explanation" cannot explain *away* the fact that he as a man of faith has received a sign of God's love, a release of God's power, or an awakening of wonder at God's activity. If the man of science cannot provide a "natural explanation", this does not make the particular events or moments any *more* religious or any more divine; it simply invites the scientific mind to continue its exploration and enquiry until perchance some "natural explanation" is discovered. Once again, the man of faith is not fearful of the results.

I believe that it was something like this that R. Bultmann was struggling to express when in an essay on "miracle" he totally rejected all attempts to relate the concept to scientific world-views, ancient or modern, and claimed that "miracle" has to do simply and solely with the response of faith made by man to God in his existential decision to accept and be in Christ. The difficulty with Bultmann's way of putting it is not in his religious insight but in his having got himself so entangled in Heideggerian philosophy that he failed to see that "miracle" *does* have something to do with the order of things with which science is concerned. A better conceptuality – dare I suggest the one which has been adopted in this book? – would have helped him to see both that science is not able to say whether this or that event *is* a "miracle", and also that the event must of necessity occur in the world with which science by its very nature has to concern itself. Although Bultmann does not talk in his essay of a "trans-natural" or "trans-historical" world and would doubtless reject such an idea with complete contempt, one cannot avoid the suspicion that something of that *heilsgeschichte* attitude is lurking somewhere in his mind. But there *is* no *heilsgeschichte*, no "salvation history" or "religious dimension" which is different from the ordinary world of events and of man's experience. It is within that *ordinary* world — which, thank heaven, is really not "ordinary" at all, but most wonderful and grand and breathtaking — that God acts, or he acts nowhere at all. Whitehead was certainly right in saying this. Yet it is in that world, just as we find it, that God shows himself in the signs that manifest his loving of men; and it is in that world, too, that those who open themselves to the cosmic Lover have released to them the power of God's love, while they find themselves now and again filled with wonder and moved to awe in the presence of "the Love that moves the sun and the other stars".

Ordinary experience, we have said, is not on a dull, dead, uniform level. There are "ups" and "downs", "mores" and "lesses", "nows" and "thens". Not only is our experience like that; so also is the world where that experience is had. It too is not dull, dead, uniform; it is no machine grinding along without excitement and thrill. What the religious and biblical meaning of "miracle" has to say to us is that in that experience and in that world, there are moments and places where in compelling fashion we are enabled to "see deeper into the heart of things". This is not as if we could draw aside a veil, once in a while, and get a glimpse of what is happening behind the world. Rather, our seeing is made possible for us as we respond in the commitment of faith to that which God is doing in the world where we are now placed.

God is the living, active, prevenient, and ceaselessly operative Love that both explains why and how things are and also discloses himself in that which he does. This is God as the biblical writers knew him and wrote about his working in the history of their own people. This is God as Jesus Christ disclosed him in the human life where our humanity was worn as a royal garment. This is the only God there is. The man who is intentionally living in relationship with God – a relationship which is always his, but which he may not "intend" in its realisation – becomes aware of this living and loving God. In that relationship there is a newly emergent level or dimension, brought to men in Jesus Christ; and when they let themselves be grasped by him, they are brought to an awareness which (as we have so often said) is both continuous with what went before, yet distinctive in its quality. *Now* the life in relationship is "life in Christ"; it is "life in love", of the quality revealed and imparted in that same Jesus Christ. Such life, Christians claim, is "life indeed".

CHAPTER SEVEN

The Point of Prayer

This chapter is not intended to provide a practical guide to prayer; for that purpose there are many books to which the reader may turn. Neither is it an introduction to that division of theology traditionally called "ascetical theology", devoted to a study of prayer from a more theoretical angle – for that purpose I should wish to recommend a little book which was published some years ago, *God in Us* by Miles Lowell Yates (S.P.C.K., 1960), to my mind the best single introduction to this subject. What we shall attempt here is something different. Our consideration of prayer will be from the more strictly systematic theological side. We shall try to relate prayer to the relationship between God and man which we have argued is the reality of Christian life; and we shall do this by looking at the basic theological affirmations which underlie all praying and which, as we shall soon see, are identical with the points to which already attention has been called. If we are at all successful in accomplishing the task which we have set ourselves, the reader will have been helped to understand what the chapter title styles "the *point* of prayer"; and he can then go on to study the principles for its exercise and the particular ways in which, as a matter of practice, he can most fruitfully engage in it.

If the main contention of this book has any validity, it is apparent that prayer like everything else in the Christian faith and life is a matter of relationship in which both sides, God *and* man, are involved. *Both* are involved; and in one sense, both are *equally* involved, since both are intent on giving and receiving. In another sense, they are *not* equally involved, since there is a difference between them. The difference is not to be found in the degree of giving and receiving, although some theologians might wish to say that; rather, it is in the question of *who* each is. Man is human, which is to say that he is "becoming" personal; he is limited, finite, and mortal. God is divine, which is to say that he is fully personal, immortal, and limited and finite only in his persisting relationships with his world. Man at the beginning of the relationship is the recipient, although later on he is able to give as well; God is always giving, from the beginning, although he is also receiving since he awaits and is affected by the response made by man.

Now it is obvious that if this matter of relationships has been correctly stated, God can be no passive, inert, unmoved recipient of our prayers. They make a *difference* to him, not only in his awareness of them but in the activity which is his true nature. What we do towards him, in thought and word and deed and *a fortiori* in our praying, counts in the working out of his purpose of good; what is more, it counts for *him* and, I dare to say, *in* him as well. It is not necessary for me to repeat what has been said earlier about the way in which God can be "enriched" by what happens in his world; all I wish to do here is to indicate that what was said earlier has most important reference to the point of prayer.

On the other hand, it is equally obvious that on this

understanding prayer cannot be seen as a purely human enterprise, in which nothing really happens from God towards man. Sometimes contemporary writers, in violent reaction from a view of prayer which appears to claim that it alters the divine purpose in its essential quality, go to the opposite extreme and say that prayer is only a matter of how man feels and thinks, with whatever consequences such feeling and thinking may have in his actions. In that case, prayer is nothing more than a rather more pious mode of thought, through which *no* changes of any kind can be achieved in the world or, of course, in God.

I believe that the reason for the errors on both sides is simply that the view of God which is taken by some theologians makes him so impassive and (if I may use this word) stolid that he resembles a self-contained and self-satisfied man of affairs who will pay no attention to anybody else. Or he is like some *thing*, an *ens* however much *realissimum* (let us again remember the neuter gender of that word *ens*), which cannot be affected by anything or anybody else. Or the view taken of man is such that he is either a passive agent of God, as if he were a puppet or marionette, jerked hither and thither according to the desires of a creator who "uses" him in pursuing ends which man has no share in achieving; or so subservient to God that he can only accept what is given him, with no hope of making his own feelings known. Worst of all, perhaps, is a view of man which fails to take any account of relationship whatsoever; in that case, man is cut off from all genuine communication with God and the best he can hope for is to have the right kind of thoughts and feelings, so that he will perhaps act in accordance with high rather than low motives.

We have seen reasons to reject all these views, both of

God and of man. Hence we are able to see that in the relationship which is prayer there is indeed a giving and a receiving, on both sides, although with the necessary qualifications which were introduced as we began our discussion. The relationship, then, is a real one between the fully personal divine Lover and the "becoming-personal" human being who was created to be a lover too.

Now in the relationship of love there is always _desire_. This can express itself in physical passion of a sexual sort. There is nothing wrong about that, even if St. Augustine, among others, seems to have regarded it as somehow part of man's sinful state and was prepared to speculate about human procreation accomplished without passion – speculation that produced some very silly remarks in the course of the _De Civitate Dei_. But desire need not always have specifically sexual expression, even if by necessity of our human makeup it must have a sexual _basis_. So much for man. As for God, it is a pity that some theologies have so _de-sexualised_ him that he cannot be thought to have desire at all, save by some remarkable exercise of double-talk which affirms of him what is at the same moment denied to him. Obviously God does not have the sexual equipment – physiological and psychological – which is part of human existence. But I am prepared to affirm that the analogue of that sexuality is part of the divine nature, however shocking to some this blunt assertion may appear. What I mean is that the passion known to us men is found in our desire to give ourselves with all our being to another who gives in return – for sexual instincts in men are _not_ simply an urge to _get_, no matter what Sartre may say; but then Sartre's notion of sexual love seems to be more like what goes on in a brothel than what goes on between ordinary men and women who love each other. This passion is also in God. He *loves* and he loves with an intensity of desire which not even the most passionate of men can equal. As our Christian faith affirms, he loves enough to give himself, in complete abandon, for the sake of his human children; that is what Jesus Christ, living and dying for us, has disclosed to men about the sort of God with whom we have to do.

I suggest that the basic point of prayer is a union of these two desires: man's desire to be fulfilled in God and God's desire to be fulfilled in man. Now if this is true, it changes our perspective on prayer from that which is so popular and conventional to one that is exciting and all-engaging. We can now see why some writers on prayer have found the marriage-symbol so helpful; and we can see why others have spoken of "the spiritual combat". Not that the latter phrase is a very good one, since to us it may suggest a kind of warfare between God and man whereas it was meant to describe a warfare between God and all that would destroy man's relationship with God – a warfare carried on in the very soul of man. Our imagery, doubtless, should be a little less violent; but whatever imagery we use it must not be of the sort which turns prayer into a tabby-cat exercise. Prayer *is* exciting; it *is* all-engaging; and it *is* a matter of what a Prayer Book collect calls "our hearty desires". There is nothing weak and enervating about *that* phrase, once we begin to take its meaning seriously.

Prayer seen in this way is very demanding. Anyone who has known what it is to be loved by another, and to love in return, is well aware of demands. The demands are never arbitrary, if the love is genuine; they speak "from deep to deep". They are both the fulfilment of our most profound need and the satisfaction of our most sincere yearning. They correspond to some reality in us which can never be adequately expressed unless it leads to a relationship in which the "I" and the "Thou" are utterly at one, not by loss of identity but by sharing in a mutual desire and willing mutually a single good.

Furthermore, in such a relationship there is pain. The pain in prayer is the pain of purgation: in Abbé Bremond's fine phrase, "the disinfection of self". It is the pain of a correction of our cheaper and easier desiring and the alignment of our genuinely "hearty desire" with the beloved and his purposes. The "grace" of love — and it *is* "grace" since all love is a gift and can never be earned by our supposed merits — is not to be had cheaply or without suffering. The Spanish proverb says that "to make love is to declare one's sorrows". Human wisdom knows this very well indeed. Divine wisdom knows it too. *God* also shares in our suffering, for he shares in our lives; yet he brings about, through the pain known in that relationship, the enrichment of our lives and uses them for the fulfilment of his purpose of love. We are glad to have it so, if we know what we are about as Christians.

But love is also joy. Through the shared suffering which it entails, the lovers come to an abiding happiness in each other and in doing each other's will. So too with respect to the relationship of God and man in prayer. There is joy here, on both sides; and the joy is shared between them. God wills for man that which in its truest intentionality is also man's will — to realise his personality, to be fulfilled, to become truly the son of God. Man wills that God's will shall be done; and he wills this not abstractly, as if from the sidelines cheering on those who are engaged in the struggle, but by giving himself utterly for that doing. When Jesus said, "Not my will, but thine, be done", he gave us the abiding illustration of this truth; and we have already stressed where the emphasis must go in that dedication of self to the heavenly Father. In the union of wills, achieved through the union of desires, there is abounding joy. Man is given a share in the "joy that is in heaven"; and the joy of God is shared with the sons of men.

This is all very well, it may be said, but what does prayer accomplish? How can I envisage the way in which prayer "works"? It has been said that prayer makes a difference to God as well as to men, but in what fashion does it make a difference? Will God *not* do good things unless men ask him? Is the divine victory contingent upon human co-operation? These are perfectly proper questions and some attempt must be made to answer them.

Once again, though, we must refer back to the *point* of prayer, which is to be found in relationship. Without that our answers will serve no purpose. We shall get nowhere; and we shall get there with astounding rapidity. It is obvious that prayer can and does produce a change in *me*. But that is not what the questions really ask about; their intention is to enquire whether anything happens in *God* — and beyond this, whether anything happens in the *world*. To our answer we shall return in a moment; but first we must say something about the change in the man who prays.

A relationship affects both partners to it, if it is a really active and living relationship. As to the human partner in this relationship which is prayer, the changes which are brought about may be seen chiefly through the effect of those aspects of prayer which include meditation, contemplation, and the like — the whole range of what is sometimes called "mental prayer" or "the higher levels of prayer". What is going on here is the direction of the total human person-in-the-making upon God himself, through various exercises and devices which are found to be effective in establishing and maintaining that kind of focussing of the attention. I look and look and look; I think and think and think . . . and the result is that I become like that which I look at and think about. "The soul", we have been told, "is dyed the colour of its leisure thoughts." That is indeed true, but it is even more true – as William James pointed out in *The Principles of Psychology*, still a valuable book, by the way, despite the great advances in psychological science since it was written – that we become like what we attend to. Prayer is classically called "the attentive presence of God"; to "attend to him", directing our thinking and looking that way, will have its profound affect on ourselves. When St. Thomas Aquinas borrowed from St. John Damascene the definition of prayer as "the elevation of the mind to God", this surely is part of what he was talking about.

Since God *is* love, the supreme cosmic Lover, to look at him with attention and to think upon him in concentration will bring about in those who engage in the practice a conformity of their "minds" – we should rather say, their whole "becoming" personalities – to God. In other words, they are started on their way to be lovers, too, or they are strengthened and increased in their capacity as lovers. The by-products of such praying, in tranquillity of soul "subsisting in the midst of endless agitation" (that was Wordsworth's fine saying), in inner peace, in the sense of assurance, in the increase in our understanding, etc., etc., are all of them related to that starting, and continuing, to reflect the vision of God as sheer Love.

So far so good. But what about God? How is *he* changed? I have already answered this question by implication in earlier pages of this book. But it may be worth repeating that God is "changed" precisely in that through his relationship with the world he is given further opportunities to create greater good and to implement such good as is already there. Such opportunities, in such ways, would not be available to him without the consentient acceptance which the world can give to him. If he were sheer coercive power, he could of course be thought to force himself upon his world, *making* it do his will; but that is not God's nature nor is it God's way of acting. As we have said, he works chiefly by persuasion, in the fullest and most intensive sense of that word. He *loves*; and there is *nothing* stronger than love, although we like to delude ourselves into thinking that "power" is stronger.

But not only is God given further opportunities to express himself in love. He is also "enriched" in his own life. As we have remarked before, this idea is often rejected as bordering on blasphemy if it is not thought to be actually indecent. Yet it is surely entailed in our taking God seriously as being nothing other than Love. Of course God does not become *more* God; he is always the supremely worshipful one and is surpassable only *by himself*. He is unchangeably *God*. But why may not the richness of what we can venture to call "God's experience" (misleading as that phrase is) be augmented? Why may not his creatures be privileged, through the very fact of their being creatures of *his*, to be the occasions for such enrichment? I can see no argument against this which is not derived from the persisting conviction that the model we must take for God is that of a self-contained and self-sufficient man who neither needs nor wants anyone to be related to him in full intimacy – with all that this signifies. It is of course entirely mistaken to caricature the position I am adopting in the

way in which John Bowden and James Richmond parody
it in their recent *Reader in Contemporary Theology* (S.C.M.
Press, 1967, p. 81) where they speak of "the 'developing'
God of process philosophy". Either they have not read
process-thinkers or they have completely misunderstood
what they have read; for no process-thinker has spoken of
"a 'developing' God". What *is* said to "develop", if that
word is allowed (and I believe it to be a most misleading
one), is the richness of the divine life as it receives into it
every contribution that the created world may provide; it
is not *God* who is developing, since *he* is always God, the
supreme all-encompassing personality who is utterly in-
surpassable by anything that is not himself.

I affirm, then, that in prayer God is actually "enriched"
by that which praying men and women undertake in this
central exercise of the God-man relationship. I affirm also
that things *do* happen in the world, as the result of prayer.
And to explain how it is possible to make such an affirmation, I must once again recall an earlier discussion. We
have insisted, it may be remembered, that temporality is
real for God as well as for man, although in God it is temporality in an eminent sense. If God were not in this sense
supremely temporal, what went on in the world would
have no meaning for him. Furthermore, it would be
utterly impossible to see how there *could* be any change in
the world due to human prayer, uniting men's "hearty"
desires with the divine love. How could that world be
changed if the deity who had it all compresent to him
would by definition also have it "all worked out" and "laid
on the line"? Classical theology has attempted to get out
of this dilemma by saying that among the things which
God in his *nunc stans* (timelessness) "knows" is that we shall
desire or ask for this and that. So those desires or askings

have already been taken into account. What is overlooked
is that prayer, in this way of seeing things, becomes merely
a formal exercise without any effective significance. But
surely this will not do. Indeed one has heard of devout
persons who, thanks to this kind of "explanation", have
felt impelled to stop praying altogether. The attempt to
explain has turned out to be a killing of "the goose that
laid the golden egg". Of course it can then be said that
God knows also that *this* man will *stop* praying; and he has
that also in his compresent awareness which is above all
time. But that sort of response is only a next step in what
becomes a *reductio ad absurdum*. The end-product, after a
long series of such steps, will be a world in which nothing
new ever happens because the God who is its "logical
explanation" *himself* does nothing. No praying Christian
can think like this; I state this bluntly and boldly, although
I know quite well that St. Thomas, for instance, did pray
– but the point about St. Thomas, as I have urged earlier,
is that he was a "double-man", one half of him being a
devout prayerful Christian whose religion was nourished
on biblical images and deep communion with the God who
was for him living and active and affected by prayer, the
other half being a philosophical theologian whose theoretical description of God contradicted what in his heart of
hearts he both believed and practised.

What I have styled God's eminent temporality has a
direct relevance to the effectiveness of prayer in doing what
we have called "changing the world". How is this? I
believe that we can begin to see light on this matter if we
pick up a phrase which was used in the preceding paragraph. There we spoke of God's "taking account of"
human desires and requests. But in *that* context the "taking
account of" was in some imagined *nunc stans*. God in his

entirely supra-temporal awareness (as well as in his "will-ing", for God is *simplex*, in classical theology, and for him to know *is* to will) was said to know what every man will desire or request, fail to desire or request; it was all *there* in God in the total simultaneity of his awareness. In our present context, however, the "taking account of" is much more seriously intended.

For I am arguing that God does *not* have it all "taped" and "laid on the line". *Of course* he knows in his wisdom all *relevant* possibilities, but in this picture he is not said to know all actually *chosen* possibilities – these are contingent and their contingency is as real to God as it is to us. *Of course* in his inexhaustible love God has the resources which will enable him to deal with any particular contingency; but those resources can only be put to work, so to say, when the contingency has occurred. When earnest prayer is made to God about this or that or cause or situa-tion, God *then* "takes account of it". As an old teacher of mine once put it, "God receives and then uses the good desires which men offer to him." In the relationship which God always has with the world, he can *now* use this "hearty desire", this urgent request from his children, in his on-going activity in that world.

Our human activity makes a difference in the way things go on; our prayers do the same. Otherwise, all petitionary and intercessory prayer is absurd and irrelevant. Yet, as William James once remarked, the odd thing about prayer is that people continue praying, no matter how the enter-prise may be "explained away". People persist in expres-sing their desires to God and they do it with some hope, perhaps fairly faint, that it counts somehow or other for them thus to express those desires. I have suggested a way in which we may make sense of that hope. But as we have seen, it entails a considerable change in our conventional picture of God as well as in our picture of the sort of world in which we live.

So far as the world is concerned, we must recognise that it is *not* a finished product. Few people perhaps think of it as such, these days, with their conscious minds; yet an enormous number still have some such idea deep down in their subconscious. If they are acquainted with scientific work, they very likely think about its "world-view" in terms of outmoded nineteenth-century mechanism or in terms of evolution taken simply as a rearrangement of what is already there. If they are of a religious turn of mind, they are the victims of that "hang-over" from deism to which I have already referred. Yet they ought to know, and to be helped to know, that modern science speaks of *epigenetic* evolution, in which new things happen. As a philosopher of our own century once said, there is "continuity of process with the emergence of genuine novelty". And religiously speaking, the deistic view was smashed to bits two hundred years ago and ought not to be permitted to linger on in some dim recesses of our minds. There is absolutely no reason whatsoever for thinking that the created order is not patient of pressures upon it, workings within it, and influences operative through it, which can and do produce fresh and unexpected events.

But, it may be asked, does this mean that even *God* can be surprised? I was once asked this question in the discussion period following a lecture. The answer which I gave began with a perhaps naughty comment: "Would you deny to *God* that which brings such delight to men?" This I meant seriously, however, despite the way in which it was said. In one sense – and here if anywhere we need to apply the Thomistic principle of *distinguo*, distinguishing among different possible meanings of a statement or a question – we can and I should claim we must allow for an element of "surprise" in God. If the particular contingency chosen by a creature is not determined and known by God, granted his awareness of the relevant possibilities in the situation, then he may be said to feel "surprise" because this rather than that possibility has been selected. Yet surprise is hardly the right word here; we might better speak of the openness of God to receive all decisions into himself and to use them for the accomplishment of his purposes, and with that openness the joy which is his as these occasions are made available to him.

But there is more to be said. Does God take up and act on every human desire expressed in prayer? Again in one sense, the answer is "Yes", since he takes each request or desire into account. But in another sense, the answer is "No", since his faithfulness in love requires that he implement only those desires or requests which are "in accordance with his will". Here we must remember that God's will is not some arbitrary fiat which bears no relationship to the fulfilment of his creatures; his will is *precisely* that fulfilment, and especially so far as man is concerned. So we may say that God takes account of *all* desires and requests, but he implements them only insofar as they contribute to the accomplishment of his purpose of love in its widest sharing. But this is only another way of saying that God *is* Love and that he abides faithful to that love which is himself. Nor is this some sophisticated variety of divine "selfishness", since what God is doing is always "for others", in whom his own joy is itself made more rich and wonderful. We could put this in an aphorism: *God* is "the *God* for others" and it is in Jesus Christ, "the *Man* for others" (in Bonhoeffer's celebrated saying), that he discloses himself as such. So there is no question of selfishness in God.

But there *may* be a question of it, so far as man is concerned. This brings us to another aspect of prayer which needs our attention. We have already quoted Abbé Bremond's fine remark about prayer as "the disinfecting of self". Surely that points to the truth. *One* of the results of praying ought to be the purification of our human desires and hence the purification of our human asking. I suspect this is why the great teachers of prayer have always been suspicious of too much emphasis on petition and intercession and too little emphasis on meditation and contemplation. They have recognised that if the former is permitted to fill the whole picture, praying may become little more than an exercise in human self-centredness in the pejorative meaning of that word. Prayer may become a continued repetition of "I, I, I", which an American poet has said is the only word heard in hell; or it may become nothing beyond an "I want, I want, I want", which Dean Inge (as we have seen) once described as a continual "pestering the deity with our petitions". Petition and intercession need purification or disinfection. The way to that is by balancing human praying with constant "recollection" of God as Love, meditating upon him as Love, and contemplating him as Love. Then the sort of petitions and intercessions we feel impelled to make will have a very different character.

There is no reason why we may not "tell God", as children sometimes put it, everything that we think we want. Since we *are* children, no matter how mature we may judge ourselves to be, that is entirely understandable and one may assume that our loving heavenly Father is delighted when his silly sons and daughters speak to him frankly and freely. But children are supposed to grow up; and we are supposed to be mature men – "in the making", of course. We are on the way to becoming personal, with all that this implies. So we should be prepared to grow in our manner of petition and intercession, as we grow in other ways. What will that mean? One thing it will most certainly mean: our praying will now be our way of identifying our own "hearty desires", and hence a way of making our requests to God, with God as himself the "pure unbounded love" of which Charles Wesley wrote and which already we have found so many occasions to stress. It will mean that more and more *our* desires will become one with God's passionate desire for good; our requests will be "according to his will", so far as we can glimpse that will in its details.

I shall bring this chapter to a conclusion by a few comments that seem to me important. The first has to do with what Père Jean de Caussade called "the sacrament of the present moment". It is in the *now* of his experience that every man must begin his praying; he has no other time in which to do it. If the relationship with God, both in its wider sense and in its more specific sense of prayer, is to have any significance it must be a *present* relationship. It is not as if one day in the future we might be related with God, nor as if back in the past we once had that relationship. "*Now* is the acceptable time." Hence praying starts from a concrete human situation and it should always be marked by a reference back to that situation. It is not in the abstract; it is in the actuality of our contemporary existence. The implications of this truth need not be pursued here; suffice it to say that they are enormous, both for the practice of prayer and for our grasp of its importance.

The second comment is related to this. The masters of prayer tell us that one of the greatest dangers in the exercise is allowing oneself to be too vague, too much inclined to "woolgathering", too lacking in concentration. Prayer is something which is *done*; it does not just "happen". Hence all the business of specific places *where* and specific times *when*, which help to overcome the temptation to shoddiness and coziness in prayer. Yet there is also a truth for which the Quietists made their stand. If they meant to say, as Molinos was accused of saying, that one should simply do nothing but be passive in the usual sense of that word, they were in effect denying all that we have insisted is the case in respect to the relationship between God and man, which is one of "fellow-working" and of "co-creation". But if they meant only that on occasion the highest activity may be an active passivity, they were entirely correct. A simple human analogy will help us here. Sometimes, when one is with a person whom one loves, one feels that the best way of "spending the time", as we put it, is just to sit quietly in the other's presence. There is no need to assume that we must be talking all the time, any more than there is any necessity for continual external activity. "I want to be there with him, just loving him." Precisely so, in human relationships; why not also in the God-man relationship in prayer? My conclusion is that prayer should include both activity and passivity (in *this* sense of the word). And that is very likely what the masters were getting at when they advocated for most people a "mixed" life of prayer itself *as well as* a "mixed" life of prayer and activity in the sense of "going about doing good".

A third comment has to do with the obvious fact that most of us some of the time, and perhaps some of us a good deal of the time, find it difficult if not impossible to maintain our praying at a high pitch of keenness and enthusiasm; there are the moments which the experts call "dryness" as well as those which might be styled "meaninglessness". Our concern here is not the practical one of giving advice to those who are troubled in praying by such experiences; it is the theological significance of these moments. We have spoken frequently of the various incognitos which God takes in his dealings with his children; we have also noted "psychological absence", when it seems that God is no longer *there* in our relationship with him — there is now only one member of what was previously a two-way contact. These two considerations are to the point here. In the difficult moments, it may well be possible to direct our thoughts to one of the divine incognitos; it may also be possible to recognise that, as we may phrase it in mythological terms, God "withdraws the sense of his presence in order that we may want him more". In any event, we are men; and that entails our physiological and psychological equipment, such as it is. Sometimes it seems that those who teach us to pray expect that we shall escape from that physiological-psychological conditioning which by definition of our manhood is inevitable. Of course we cannot make any such escape. It would be a theological error to talk as if we could; and in the present discussion of God's relationship with man, and man's with God, we have seen that there is every reason against falling into that error.

Prayer is frequently divided into certain elements: for example, vocal prayer including petition, intercession, confession, thanksgiving, adoration; and mental prayer including meditation, various kinds of contemplation, and mystical union. There is nothing wrong with such divisions, provided they are not thought to be exclusive one of the others and provided that people are not supposed to engage in each of them successively in a certain routine fashion. But there is a theological reason for refusing to make these divisions *too neat and precise*. In prayer we have a relationship between God and man; it is a relationship in love. Rules may be helpful on occasion; distinctions may sometimes be illuminating in respect to ways in which this and that mode of love's expression may appropriately be implemented at a particular time. But love cannot be tied down to rules and it is inclined to laugh at precise distinctions. There is a glorious spontaneity about love which rejects all attempts to regulate it and to make it follow some prescribed scheme. One suspects that this obvious fact in all human loving is equally true of the love between God and man known in the relationship established by our creation and given its distinctive quality in Jesus Christ.

Theologically speaking, anything which would damage that spontaneity, with its openness and delight, between God and man is to be regarded with more than suspicion; it is, in fact, likely to prove disastrous to the human member of the relationship. As to what it means to God, one cannot say, but one suspects that it may be an occasion for sorrow to the God whose innermost heart is laid bare in the human life of Jesus.

I wish to end this chapter with two quotations. The first is from a short piece written some years ago by the Reverend Raymond Efemey and published in *The Church Times* newspaper for August 20th 1965. I quote the passage because it has to do with the relation of the experience of *human* loving, with its inevitable sexual associations, to the love of God as he has disclosed himself to us in Christ. Mr. Efemey writes: "I think the Beatles are terrific – amusing, sensual and yet tender – enthusiastic, full of vigour, possessing sometimes moments of real beauty. I am quite unashamed of this, especially since I realised one day how all that natural virility could be applied, just how their songs *could* be sung:

> 'She loves you, and you know that can't be bad;
> She loves you, and you know you should be glad!'

"Before you collapse with either laughter or disgust, will you compare the two following quotations?

> 'When someone really loves you,
> That's when your life begins.'

> 'Sick with love am I,
> And naught can cure my ill
> Save only if of thee I have my fill.'

[The first couplet is from Brian Poole and the Treme-loes,* the second from St. John of the Cross.]

"It all depends on how you look at it, doesn't it? God really does mean us to find him adorable with every part of that complicated mechanism we call our personality."

This quotation seems to me to be both existentially moving and theologically of great importance. It is surely unnecessary to point its moral for our discussion of prayer, beyond saying that Mr. Efemey's insistence on the whole personality in its relationship with God is a splendid confirmation of one of the main emphases in this book. Nowhere is it more relevant than in respect to prayer, which so often has been regarded as somehow eviscerated,

---

* Reproduced by kind permission of Burlington Music Company Ltd.

inhuman, escapist, and only possible for persons who are not warm-blooded modern men and women but really belong in Victorian stained-glass windows.

In the course of our discussion of providence in human life we had occasion to make an extended quotation from Dr. DuBose, the American Anglican theologian whose remarkable penetration has only recently been recognised – although he died in the second decade of this century after teaching for nearly fifty years at the University of the South in Tennessee. In the same book from which our earlier quotation was taken Dr. DuBose has a brief but invaluable section on his own change of mind in respect to prayer. After years of praying, and thinking about prayer, he reached the conclusion which I now reproduce in full. "[In prayer] there are two ways of God, or two modes of the one way: First, he will not change nature for us, but he will, if we love him and enter into his purpose, make everything in nature, the good and the evil, good to us, work together for our good. I do not mean that he will do this merely by fitting or adjusting us to things as they are, but that he will make the things, whatever they are, actual instruments and ministers of our good . . . And second, I do not say that God will not change nature, do away with natural evils and provide natural goods, but only that he will not do it for us, in the sense of instead of us. He will not do it magically or miraculously . . . There is absolutely no limit to what he will do through us and by us in these ways if we will be workers with him for good. God does not want to put away our sin by magic, he wants us to put it away by holiness; and so he does not work upon us by miracle, but works in us by grace; which means that he calls and moves and enables us to put away our sin by repentance and to put on holiness and life by faith . . .

What he wants is not the work but the working and the workers, the love that bears all, believes all, endures and survives all, accomplishes all, and so at last becomes and is all. And so what do we come at last to pray for, and how? By 'at last' I mean when we have passed beyond praying for things as we think we want them and come to take them as God knows we want them . . . I pray to God only for God, to Christ only for Christ, to the Holy Ghost only for the Holy Ghost, and for everything else natural and spiritual only as through them and by them God will give me himself."

CHAPTER EIGHT

What It All Comes To

In this concluding chapter we shall round out our discussion by giving attention to various matters that for one reason or another have not been considered in the course of this book. Then we shall attempt to make some very simple practical applications of what *has* been said. The former considerations are required in order to leave as few loose bits as possible; the latter for another reason which must be put briefly.

This volume is in a series called The Library of *Practical* Theology. I have italicised this adjective because it states the point that I wish to make. Theology as such is the attempt to systematise and order, in some intelligible and coherent fashion, the deliverances of religious experience as they are related to and illuminate all the other areas of man's life in this vast world. How we interpret what we have just called "religious experience" will depend upon our particular stance, religiously speaking. We may wish to emphasise revelation in act; or we may wish to stress the profound differences which faith makes; or we may prefer to start from the world at large as men interpret it in the light of some deep moments in which (as they think) its significance has been made plain to them. Whatever their starting point, theology always seems to show a tendency

to become somewhat academic, not only because the doing
of theology has so largely been in the hands of academi-
cally minded people but also because a certain precision
of thought and care in expression are demanded in the
attempt at theological construction.

All this is true and to be expected. Every statement of
the meaning of human activity, when examined and
ordered, tends in this direction. But at the same time, the
theological enterprise can never be unrelated to *life*. It
derives from that which living men and women believe,
say, and do; and it refers back to those same men and
women. In this sense, all theology is a matter of "know-
how", as the phrase goes today. And it does mean that
whatever is said theologically must have genuine relevance
to the living of human life in faith and by grace. Any theology that does not have such a relevance, however remote
the relevance may on occasion seem to be, is a theology
which stands self-condemned – or if not self-condemned,
it remains as primarily a matter of speculation which has
little possibility of genuine verification beyond possessing
logical consistency, schematic coherence, and such occasional proper reference to philosophy and science as
may be claimed for it.

It has been my purpose in this book to speak of God and
man, brought together in Jesus Christ; of the continuing
relationship of God and man; and of the particular topics
of providence, the "miraculous", and prayer; and to
speak in such a fashion that the thoughtful yet not theologically expert believer can find that these things have to
do with *him* – with him as he seeks to live Christianly in
this present world. Furthermore, it has been my hope that
what is said in this book will present to the unbeliever, the
agnostic, and the man or woman who is only "interested

in what Christians have to say", something of the richness
of Christian thinking and something of the motivation as
well as the enabling which Christian faith provides for
those who hold it. How successful I have been is not for me
to say. This at least has been my intention and my desire.

Therefore, in the last pages of this chapter we shall
speak in what could be called a very *practical* way about
how Christian living is an expression of the relationship
with God which Jesus Christ is believed to have established; and how within that relationship it is also an
expression of active trust in God's providential "govern-
ance", to use a Kierkegaardian noun, as well as in his
special actions that reveal and release his goodwill or love;
and also how such living requires, for its fullest sharing,
the conscious and intentional times of "waiting upon God"
that go by the name of prayer.

For the present, however, we must turn to the discussion
of two or three matters that may need some clearing up.

One of these has to do with man's place in this enormous world. There was a time when it was believed that
the planet upon which we live was at the very centre of the
cosmos; we no longer believe that. But the dislodgement
of the earth from that central position has not altered
another idea which still persists in many Christian quar-
ters. This is that *man himself* is at the centre of things. What
goes on in his life is all that matters ultimately, it may be
thought; in the great world, suns and stars and the rest of
the creation exist only in order to provide a stage upon
which the human drama is played out. The more thoughtful of us do not really believe this any more; yet a good
deal of our conventional religious talk still moves in the
realm where such an idea is implied.

It is by now more than plain that the position presupposed in this book is theistic, but with a difference from much in "classical theism". That difference is found in an insistence on what Hartshorne has called "the bi-polarity" of God, so that the divine attributes such as his power, his wisdom, and his love are always to be subjected to a double analysis. Thus he is one "whose power, while unsurpassable, is social; whose wisdom, while perfect, is ever changing; and whose love, while constant, is pure sensitivity to creativity, joy, and sorrow". The quotation is taken from an excellent brief study of process-theology by Dr. E. H. Peters (*The Creative Advance*, 1966). In such a conception there is no reason whatever to reject the possibility of many most varied ways in which God may work in his world, quite apart from the human enterprise which is the one that we ourselves know at first hand.

When we remember the vastness of the universe as astronomical investigation has disclosed it to us, the enormous time-span of which we have become more and more conscious, and the infinitesimally small as well as the overwhelmingly great in the cosmos, it is entirely possible for us to accept the view that the range of the divine activity includes much that we can never know. In ways beyond our human understanding "God is working his purpose out", as the hymn puts it. What God is "up to" elsewhere in the universe is not for us to know, at least at this point in man's pilgrimage on earth. This will include, at levels below man, the relevant occasions for the expression of his purpose of goodness; for, as we have argued in a note appended to an earlier chapter, it is absurd to suppose that only in the realm of history and human affairs is there any divine self-manifestation. Nature is much more than the background for the human drama, although that was how it must have seemed to many in the past. Yet the

Bible never regards it in that way – "the heavens declare the glory of God; and the firmament sheweth his handy-work", says the Psalm; and this is not only for *man's* sake, but because God in his infinite richness always seeks and finds ways in which he may express himself for good.

But there is more to be said. God is the creative agency in the world; he is both causative and affective. He is also the "chief exemplification" (in Whitehead's phrase) of all principles necessary to describe that world. Hence as the *chief* exemplification and the *ultimate* source of creativity, he is the creator (*not* the artificer, but the artist or poet) and the redeemer (the one who saves all that can be saved) of the world, as we have presupposed and on more than one occasion explicitly indicated. *God* is the centre of the cosmos, not man. And God most probably has many other purposes which he is working out, quite beside the pur-poses he entertains for human life. Some glimpse of those other purposes may very well be granted us now and again; but for the most part we are ignorant of them. Should there be other planets which have rational crea-tures upon them, God must have some aim for those crea-tures. He must also have some aim in respect to every level of the many-sided and many-dimensioned process in which we play our small part. There is nothing sub-Christian or un-Christian in saying things of this sort. It is only our inveterate anthropocentrism which makes us afraid of them – nothing religiously significant is here involved.

Yet it *is* essential to Christian faith to maintain that whatever God is "up to" elsewhere than in human life, and wherever he is operating in other places than those known to us, *all* of his working is "of one substance with" that which goes on for men. It is *all* the activity of the God who is "pure unbounded love"; and therefore we need have no fear that in some corner of the universe a quite different activity is in process – one of evil, say, or of a *kind* of good that is in outright contradiction to that which is known here in our human experience. Greater, more wonderful, differing in many respects, appropriately related to other conditions and situations: all this, of course. But it is of a piece with the love which in Jesus Christ is disclosed in action for our wholeness of life. This is the first point to be stressed.

A second follows from it. Since we do not know the way in which God's purpose of good is expressed and active elsewhere, save by such glimmerings as may be granted us or such assurance of congruity as Christian faith demands, *our* job is to get on with our own living in relationship with God. In this sense, Voltaire's Candide was entirely correct, *il faut cultiver notre jardin*. We may enjoy speculation and we may indulge in theorising, but the *job* for us is to see to it that human life is patterned in terms of the love which is God's purpose for *us*, both as those who are on the way to becoming personal and as those who in this way are knit together with their fellows in the bundle of life which is human existence. This means that there is a certain fitting humility in the undertaking of the human enterprise as a whole. What we know, we know; what we may be led to know more fully, that we shall know more fully. This is no appeal to sanctified ignorance nor to the silly rejection of the spirit of exploration; but it is an insistence that we do not pretend to be wiser than we are; and coupled with that, an insistence that the Christian's main concern is with "doing the will of God" in the immediate here-and-now where he is placed.

The third and last matter which needs tidying up has to do with the non-Christian religions and the possibility of further revelation from God of his nature and purpose. As to the former, it would be blasphemous simply to condemn those other ways in which men have sought divine truth as being only a great mass of error and an entirely perverted expression of the religious instinct. What von Hügel called "God-given graces and mercies" are found in many strange places and among many people who have never heard the name of Jesus Christ. It is no part of the Christian task to deride and denounce those places, save when they contain elements that are positively harmful to man's fulfilment in community. It *is* the Christian task to share the qualitatively distinctive life with God in Christ; and to share it with as many people as can be brought to accept and live it. Then, and then only, will whatever is erroneous or imperfect and perhaps terribly distorted in religious traditions other than Christian be shown for what it is. At the same time the truth and beauty present in such traditions will shine the more brilliantly once they have been brought into relationship with the focal self-disclosure of God in the event of Christ himself.

As to the possibility of further revelation, no man can say that God has ceased or ever will cease to reveal himself to his human children. Precisely *because* he is the supreme cosmic Lover, who has acted in Christ, "there is yet more truth and light to break forth from his most holy word". Sometimes the thought is expressed that another revelation will come along – this is the way it is usually said – which will supplant and replace Jesus. But how could he be supplanted and replaced if what is disclosed in him is *the truth* about God and man in their relationship? Can we say more, or even envisage the possibility that more could be said, than that God is always and everywhere the Lover of men; that men are made to be lovers too; that their relationship is shared love in that mutuality of giving and receiving which love essentially signifies; and that in the One whom Christians accept as Brother and Lord this relationship came to a focus, so that the rays of God's loving activity were in him concentrated as in a burning-glass? This is *decisive* precisely because it opens the door to endless development; it is *definitive* precisely because it points the direction of advance; and it is *crucial* because it makes plain that "at the ending of our day, we shall be judged by our loving", in the noble words first spoken by St. John of the Cross.

We may now return to those practical applications which are essential if theology is to be living reality and not an interesting but perhaps idle speculation.

Samuel Taylor Coleridge, in *Aids to Reflection*, wrote these words: "Christianity is not a Theory, or a Speculation; but a *Life*; not a *Philosophy* of Life, but a Life and a Living Process. Its proof lies in the trial: 'Try it.' " My first point is that because of the relationship between God and men which is established for us, in its peculiarly distinctive quality, in Jesus Christ, we are engaged as Christians in "a life and a living process". Since that is the case, the demonstration of the reality of Christianity is not speculative nor purely logical, but overwhelmingly vital and experimental. I have never seen this so admirably stated as by David Jenkins in his recent Bampton Lectures: "The end of the argument . . . will come, I believe, only when we are brought to that perfected community which is the fulfilment of humanness through Jesus Christ in the reality of God himself. Only then may we hope to know for certain both what the truth really is and that such truth truly exists. Meanwhile, I suggest that in living by faith we are, in fact, arguing for and searching for truth.

The peculiar nature of the faith which is response to the reality in Jesus Christ is the assurance that the truth for which we seek has already sought and found us. The peculiar danger of faith is to pervert this assurance into a self-centred conviction that we have found the truth. So we can seek because we have been found and are ourselves committed to putting whatever we find at the service of and to the test of further seeking. This is the experiment which is living . . . The only experiment which gives room enough for truly human living is the experiment into God. Further, this is the experiment which is both possible and has every hope of a successful outcome because a proper understanding of the things concerning Jesus gives us reason to believe that God has undertaken the experiment of being a man." (*The Glory of Man*, p. 117).

That is very finely said. And for our purposes it means that if we hope ever to grasp what is intended by talk of God's care for his children, his giving us special occasions for knowing his love and power, and our awareness of the significance of the intentional communion with him which is prayer, *we must make precisely this "experiment"* – in Coleridge's words, we must "try it".

Here is no short range pragmatism, in which immediate results are to be found or else the enterprise will be given up as futile. On the contrary, this is what von Hügel called "long range" pragmatism or "fruitfulness", if that is the right phrase; in such increasing "fruitfulness and richness", as von Hügel also noted, we have pointers towards truth. Nor does this mean that the intellectual task is entirely abrogated so that we are to believe "anything that comes down the road", as a friend of mine once put it. Again on the contrary, it demands the fullest use of such powers of reason as may be ours; but with the use of that reason, the commitment which is faith. This requires the outstretching of our whole being, in an imaginative move- ment of self, that will justify the definition once given of faith: "reason grown courageous" and hence reason pre- pared to go beyond the immediate knowledge which we think that we possess.

This brings me to my second point. *The thing takes time.* Dean Inge remarked on one occasion that no one who had honestly and with utter dedication given himself to God "ever came away empty". But the dedication is not for a brief trial only; it is *for always*, as the Americans say. Just as in the relation of man and woman, the promise of faith- fulness is "till death us do part" – i.e., a lifelong engage- ment of person with person; so in the Christian experiment the undertaking is intended to be permanent and unceas- ing. Otherwise we can have no hope of "tasting and seeing that the Lord is gracious".

Thirdly, the particular way in which each man will enter upon the God-man relationship by his surrender in faith will doubtless differ from the way appropriate for another man. There is a special *attrait* for each man; von Hügel was accustomed to place great emphasis on this, saying that each of us is to follow that "drawing" to God in Christ which is right for *him*, neither seeking another way nor criticising his fellows because they do not follow the one that is right for *him*. The remarkable variety of "holiness" found in the saints whom the Christian Church honours is a demonstration of this diversity in unity. It would be very hard to find much in common between, say, St. Francis of Assisi, St. John of the Cross, George Herbert, and John Wesley, save for one thing: their common dedication to the love of God in Christ Jesus and their astounding reflec- tion of that love in their own human loving.

A fourth point to which attention must be called is that the language in which this relationship is described will vary from man to man and from place to place, as well as from time to time. *How* one may speak of the awareness of God's providential care, and of the special moments of God's activity upon us and in us, and of the mode of union called prayer, will depend upon one's own time and place. Because we belong to a great company of the faithful, each of us will be taught by the Church's past; yet each of us also will have his own way of thinking and speaking, his own language. This is not only explained by the enormous richness of that reality about which we speak; it is also explained by our own human differences. Therefore we can be ready to welcome novel, fresh, perhaps surprising ways of talking about the enduring Christian life in Christ. We must expect that theology itself will be a developing "science", not a static once-for-all description of what Christianity is all about.

To say this is also to say the fifth thing in these practical considerations. That is to emphasise the necessity, for every man who gives himself to this "experimental" relationship, of combining faithfulness to the old with openness to the new. The faithfulness to the old demands that we shall be prepared always to listen to our fathers in Christian faith and living. As G. K. Chesterton said, "to give them a vote" in such matters means precisely that we *do* listen to them. At the same time, we look towards the future. Living towards the future, the existentialists tell us, is the peculiar characteristic of human living when it is authentic and not reduced simply to sheer undifferentiated "man-ness". *Dasein* (*this* man-ness) in all its particularity, says Heidegger, delivers us from being just *man*; and part of that particularity is to live towards the future, to live in

12

expectation of great things to come, speaking to us from what G. M. Hopkins so beautifully called "the dearest freshness deep down things".

Finally, the practical significance of everything that has been said is found in our readiness to *act*. Christian living is no "cloistered virtue", kept to ourselves in our secret heart and never expressed in that which we *do*. In the fourth gospel, much is made about "doing the truth" (3.21). For the evangelist, faithful as he was to his Jewish inheritance, truth was never a matter of possession – as if one had been permitted to have some privileged insight into reality. It was always a matter of action. This is why he portrays Jesus as telling his compatriots that if they did not happen to believe in him for any other reason, at least "for the very works' sake" (14.11) they could believe. What Jesus *did* was what Jesus *was*. If we wish to put it so, we can say that any sound christology must be a functional christology; nor does this contradict the ontological reality which must also be asserted. The "ontology" of the incarnate life is *in* its functioning, as we began this book by insisting.

There is no necessary contradiction between "functional" and "ontological", either in Christ himself nor in the world. There may seem to be so, if we take for our metaphysical starting-point the concept of "being" or "completely fulfilled actuality" or *ens realissimum*. But if we begin with a recognition that "becoming" is a more inclusive term than "being", the situation is quite different. In that case, the proper meaning of "being" is the guarantee of consistency and the faithfulness to which we have referred so often. But what *is*, in that sense, is a living, moving, dynamic process – a development towards ends that will satisfy each occasion within the process and also satisfy the process as a whole. This carries with it a corollary: that in at least one definition of the term, there is no "end"; there is no *finis*, when creative advance comes to a full stop. We have seen reason to think that even classical Christian theology does not demand a beginning and an end, in such a definition of the terms. There is every reason to think, in the light of all that we now know, that the creative process is *everlasting*. From it, as it proceeds, the divine creative reality, which is nothing other than the cosmic Lover, secures his own satisfaction which is not for himself only but shared with his world. There is no occasion which does not have that Lover as its inescapable *prius*; this is the truth in the concept of *creatio ex nihilo*, once we have "demythologised" it and understood that its point is not in some moment when for the first time the world came into being. It is also possible to say that there is a continuing *consummation* of all things, since at every instant God is both extracting from the world that which is valuable in it, including its own creation of goods through the exercise of responsible freedom, and employing those valuable goods for further advance in his aim of sharing more fully the love which is his very essence. Thus it might be said that "being" is adjectival to "becoming", rather than the other way round as classical theism has sought to claim.

In any event, so far as God is concerned, the scriptural portrayal of his mode of revelation is always in these dynamic terms. We know what he *is* (which is to say, we know his character, his purpose, his innermost quality), and hence we know the world itself (which is to say, ourselves, our history, the natural order in all its wonder), through what God *does*. Or as we began this book by saying, God's *self-disclosure in act* is theologically crucial.

Someone has remarked that God's language is "verbs" not "nouns". I should wish to qualify this a little by noting that verbs always have a substantival signification, even when they are not necessarily concerned with what an older theology called "substances". By this I mean that to speak of *activity* is always to speak of a "routing of actual occasions" (in Whitehead's language) which is knit together into an ongoing entity that can be spoken about as a *this* or a *that*, or in God's and man's case a *who*. Yet it remains true that God's way of making himself known to us is through what he does. He does not reveal himself to us by dropping down from heaven a series of theological truth-statements or moral judgements. Hence in *our* sharing in the relationship with him, we must *act*.

In the particular issues with which we have been concerned, we can see that action is always involved. If we are talking about God's providential care of his children in this world, we are speaking not only of what *God* does for them and in them, but also of what *they* do as they make their response in life to that which happens towards them. The religious significance of what we call the "miraculous" is seen, once again, in that which *God* does towards men; yet it is also seen only when *men* act too – for in the gospels we read that *active faith* was the condition for the reception of this gracious power and for the recognition that in this or that given instance God's goodness and love were disclosed.

Above all, *prayer* is an act. We have seen that much of the time, the act of prayer is an *active* passivity, a "waiting upon *God*". But we have also seen that such passivity is not equivalent to inertia; on the contrary, to "recollect" means actively to bring all of ourselves together so that we may concentrate upon God. I recall an old friend of mine saying once that the closest analogy he knew to "contemplative prayer" was an occasion when he took his son to see a locomotive in a railway station. "The boy looked and looked at it in wonder and delight," he said. Then he added, "He wasn't *doing* anything but looking, and yet he was the most *active* boy I've ever seen." In all its ranges, prayer is activity, even when the activity is not a matter of feverish external behaviour.

We have come to the end of this study of "God's way with men". In briefest summary, we may say that this is a way of relationship, in which God's human children are caught up into a love that holds them forever; in which they know a love to which they are impelled to respond. It is a love which, because they respond by opening themselves to the fullest degree, is then released through them into the world to touch the lives of others. In living in such relationship, these sons of men are brought also to know the care which the cosmic Lover has for them and exercises upon them. They know the occasional moments when, as so inadequately and misleadingly we are obliged (by the limitations of our human language) to phrase it, the Lover "breaks through" to them in a strangely compelling fashion. And they know the sense of fellowship with that Lover, in an openness which in particular ways they consciously and intentionally will in what the great teachers of prayer have called "the attentive presence of God". All of it springs from love; all of it returns to love: all of it expresses love. Perhaps that is why a nineteenth-century writer was not entirely wrong when he said of the Church:

"... not *credo* then,
Amo shall be the password through her gates."

Index

(NOTE: Recurrent topics, e.g., God as Love, Divine Disclosure in Act, etc., are not noted in this index. Neither are the three main subjects, Providence (Chapter V), Miracle (Chapter VI), and Prayer (Chapter VII), since the discussion of these is concentrated in the chapters mentioned.)

DATE DUE